New Philadelphia

by Gerald A. McWorter
and Kate Williams-McWorter
for the New Philadelphia Association
Path Press, Inc. 2018

Copyright © 2018 by Gerald A. McWorter and Kate Williams-McWorter. All rights reserved. No part of this book may be reproduced, stored in a retrieval system, or transmitted in any form by any means, electronic, mechanical, photocopying, recording, or otherwise without prior written permission, except in the case of brief quotations embodied in critical articles or reviews.

For more information on the cover photograph, see page 122.

Cataloging-in-Publication data
Names: McWorter, Gerald A., author | Williams-McWorter, Kate (1958-), author.
Title: New Philadelphia / Gerald A. McWorter and Kate Williams-McWorter
Description: Evanston, Illinois: Path Press Inc. 2018 | 211 pages: illustrations, maps; 23 cm | Includes bibliographical references (pages 201-211).
Identifiers: LCCN 2018023328 | ISBN 9780910671170 | ISBN 0910671176
Subjects: LCSH: New Philadelphia (Ill.)—History. African Americans—Illinois—History. Frank, Free (1777-1854). Underground Railroad. Community life—Illinois—New Philadelphia—History.
Classification: LCC F549.N49 M39 2018 | DDC 977.3/453

Designed by Rachel Guthrie
Printed in the United States of America

Send inquiries to:
Path Press, Inc.
Post Office Box 5683
Evanston, Illinois 60204
pathpressinc@aol.com

Table of Contents

- Introduction 1
- CHAPTER ONE: NEW PHILADELPHIA IN UNITED STATES HISTORY . 9
- CHAPTER TWO: FOUNDING FAMILY 31
- CHAPTER THREE: TOWN 67
- CHAPTER FOUR: SETTLEMENT 99
- CHAPTER FIVE: MEMORY 131
- CHAPTER SIX: REBIRTH 157
- Epilogue 193
  - Appendix 195
  - Works consulted 201

From Ensign 1872, page 84. Public domain.

Introduction

New Philadelphia is a place and an experience that has endured for more than 180 years. Its physical space is in west-central Illinois, but its memory has reached around the world through the remarkable work of its early settlers, the strong ties of their descendants, the sustained efforts of modern-day local residents and scholars, and finally recognition by the federal government. New Philadelphia was founded as a town in 1836 and continued as an informal settlement beginning in 1885, but its identity took shape before 1836 and continues today. New Philadelphia is an American story that reveals the historic nature of freedom, the strength of family, the possibility of managing racism and violence against African Americans in a stable community, and the importance of establishing a cultural heritage upon which to build the future.

This story is important for many reasons. On the one hand it is a unique story of the accomplishments of several African American families and their experiences in an integrated community. This was a community led by the McWorter family, a community based on an abolitionist mission, to free African Americans from the bondage of slavery. In this way it is a universal story of freedom. The main message for today is that if New Philadelphia was possible, and if we can learn the lessons it has to teach us, then the experiment that is the United States of America might actually work. Langston Hughes said it clearly in his visionary appeal for change:

> O, let America be America again—The land that never has been yet—And yet must be—the land where *every* man is free. The land that's mine—the poor man's, Indian's, Negro's, ME—Who made America, Whose sweat and blood, whose faith and pain, Whose hand at the foundry, whose plow in the rain, Must bring back our mighty dream again. (Hughes 1938, page 9)

This story of New Philadelphia is presented in historical stages that help to place it in the narrative of the United States and the world. Two things often go unmentioned in historical narratives. One, the United States was founded as a settler colony based on the genocidal extermination of the people who were here before the Europeans. Two, African Americans played an active role in shaping United States history, especially through their fight for freedom. It is impossible to tell the story of New Philadelphia without challenging and ending these silences.

The first stage of New Philadelphia, Native America, lasted for centuries and included the Meskwaki or Fox, the Kickapoo, and Illinois groups such as the Peoria, Kaskaskia, and Cahokia. Illinois River Potawatomi lived a little further north and east. At least two renowned chiefs died fighting for their right to remain in and around New Philadelphia: Chief Senachwine in 1831 and Chief Black Hawk in 1838.

This stage ends with the arrival of settlers from the east. Two of these were to make their mark on the area along with the residents of New Philadelphia, namely, Abraham Lincoln, who migrated to Illinois as a young man, and Samuel Clemens, whose family settled in nearby Missouri where he was born in 1835 and grew up, later taking the pen name Mark Twain.

The second stage of New Philadelphia, Family, centers on the McWorters led by Frank McWorter or "Free Frank." Apart from the generations of Native Americans, Frank was the first to settle there, helped by his wife who was known as "Free Lucy." As one 1967 history book put it, "The first white man to settle Hadley Township was a colored man." (Thompson 1967, page 151) Frank was born a slave in South Carolina in 1777 and grew up in Kentucky, where he was able to "hire out," in other words, he put in additional hours after working full-time on his owner's plantation and keep all or part of the money he earned. By 1817 he was able to buy freedom for the most important family member: his wife Lucy, pregnant with their fifth child Squire. So began decades of work and planning, enabling Frank to buy his own freedom and that of 15 other family members.

He eventually sold everything he owned in Kentucky, particularly a saltpeter mine, for a tract of land in Pike County, Illinois, sight unseen. Frank McWorter and his family arrived on this land in 1831. They cleared the land to begin living on it and farming, and the idea to found a town took shape.

New Philadelphia's third stage of life, Town, spanned 50 years. In 1836, five short years after the McWorters arrived, Frank had the land mapped into town lots and registered as a town in the county seat of Pittsfield, Illinois. New Philadelphia became an active, integrated abolitionist town with a post office, a school, a store, a blacksmith, two shoemakers, and various prosperous farming families. In 1841, Squire McWorter wrote to his brother "Frank, Jr." in Canada, "We have at present a school in Philadelphia and Commodore and Anna have been going most of the time since it commenced," and in another letter, "Commodore has got to be a pretty good gunner he has killed six deer he likes hunting very well... [N]ew towns and roads are multiplying all over the country[.] Alonzo Love talks of setting up the blacksmiths business in the town of Philadelphia." Blacksmiths and shoemakers almost certainly figured into the tale passed down the generations that said, "Get you to New Philadelphia and those McWorter boys'll help you get a horse and a pair of shoes and on your way to Canada."

New Philadelphia occupations reported in the census for the years 1850-1880 and summarized in Charlotte King's 2003 undergraduate thesis include three schoolteachers, two shoemakers, two blacksmiths, Baptist preacher, cabinetmaker, merchant, wheelwright, carpenter, physician, farm workers, coal miner, minister, seamstress, shop worker, speculator, storekeeper, house servant, as well as farmers, farmworkers, and laborers. (King 2003) An analysis of the United States and Illinois censuses of the time shows that the population in and very near New Philadelphia rose as high as 160 people living in 29 households. Families farming in the area also relied on the town.

Up through the Civil War (1861-1865), New Philadelphians fought for freedom in seven ways. First, they worked their way, carving minerals from underground, coaxing crops from the soil, raising animals, selling what they could, including the land itself. Second, they ran from slavery. Third, several families bought family members out of slavery in Kentucky and Missouri and perhaps elsewhere. Fourth, they continually helped others seeking freedom, and the town they founded became known as a station on the Underground Railroad. Fourth, they named the town after the nation's first City of Brotherly Love, that center of antislavery activity, Philadelphia, Pennsylvania. This gave a definite signal as to the spirit of the place. Sixth, townspeople sent their sons into the Civil War, fighting separately in either colored or white units. Seventh and most basically, African Americans and Europeans all lived free, in this integrated town, a few miles from the slave market in Hannibal, Missouri. In other words, here Black people owned land and had guns, 20 miles from the Mississippi River, that renowned boundary and thoroughfare for both slavery and freedom. New Philadelphia was a town founded on the desire for freedom and the willingness to fight for it.

The fourth stage of New Philadelphia, Settlement, began with an ending: in 1885 a legal order converted taxable town lots back into taxable farmland. Other rural towns were also losing official recognition and/or social existence as the population left to seek work in the nation's growing industrial cities; post offices, stores and other services closed; and land lived on was gradually returned to farmland. But the New Philadelphia area remained an integrated settlement of European Americans and African Americans, a community of farming families. At a time when the national norm was segregated schools, Black and white children alike attended New Philadelphia School, built on land donated by the McWorter family, until school consolidation in 1948. The market life of the residents shifted to the nearest surviving town of Barry, Illinois. Railroads crisscrossed Pike County helping move the agricultural products to bigger markets.

Arthur McWorter raised his five children on his grandfather Frank's New Philadelphia farm—worked continuously by four generations—and then in his old age followed his children to Chicago.

The Burdick family, having arrived in the 1800s, farmed and lived in and around the former town until the 1970s. Their barn, chicken coop, and the last house they built are three of the seven structures now on the New Philadelphia lots that were platted in 1836.

The power of New Philadelphia is that even as the settlement dwindled, it lived on into a fifth stage, that of Memory. This has included the New Philadelphia family networks that spread across the United States from Texas to Alaska, Washington DC to California. They continued to treasure and retell their experiences. McWorter descendants in Illinois made annual pilgrimages back to their ancestral home and participated in local cultural activities such as the annual Barry Apple Festival. But others also remembered New Philadelphia. Other Pike County families, many of them longtime farmers, carried memories from their ancestors. History buffs retold the story. Local historical societies published the story, as did Pike County newspapers and other Illinois media, particularly the *Chicago Defender*. The Barry Historical Museum kept and displayed clippings and photographs.

People were so determined that New Philadelphia would be remembered that they returned to the physical place for help. We all know how place helps you remember. Returning to your childhood home ... landing back in your hometown ... walking a long familiar street ... all these things bring memories flooding back. The place was the New Philadelphia cemetery. Arthur's oldest daughter, Thelma, and her daughter Juliet Walker, born in Chicago, took up the cause of getting the grave of "Free Frank" McWorter onto the National Register of Historic Places, and in 1988 they succeeded. Juliet walked from Kentucky to Illinois to draw attention to the official recognition, and arrived in Barry just in time for a local ceremony celebrating the occasion.

Truly, all the memory-keeping up to that point made possible the current stage, Rebirth. And Rebirth has in turn bolstered and spread the memory and stories of New Philadelphia.

The Rebirth stage has involved many people in activities in and around the physical place of the former abolitionist town. By the

1990s, as the county saw the arrival of the interstate highway, additional work began to renew the place always known as New Philadelphia.

The New Philadelphia Association (NPA) itself emerged as planning and construction of Interstate 72 ended. The NPA was sparked and sustained by broad local interest in preserving the town site and the McWorter family cemetery, both located near the new highway. The NPA reached out to others, among them scholars and town descendants. NPA has been the primary advocate for New Philadelphia for more than two decades. This book is just one of their latest projects.

The rebirth of New Philadelphia was possible because the story is powerful and memories and documentation were intact. Local residents mobilized. Scholars from the University of Illinois, the University of Maryland, and the Illinois State Museum were able to obtain National Science Foundation funding. Partnering with the NPA and others, they carried out several years of history and archaeology research and teaching at the site.

On August 11, 2005, the town site itself was added to the U.S. National Register of Historic Places. On January 16, 2009, the New Philadelphia Town Site was designated a National Historic Landmark. In 2013, the National Park Service recognized New Philadelphia as a station on the Underground Railroad and included it in the NPS Network to Freedom. In 2014, President Obama signed a bill authorizing the National Park Service to study New Philadelphia's potential as a national park. (It was the New Philadelphia, Illinois, Study Act numbered H.R. 930 and S. 1328, and was ultimately included in the National Defense Authorization Act for 2015.)

But more important than the uniqueness of New Philadelphia is this: it is an example of the remembering that every community needs. Every pre-Civil War community of free African Americans can be remembered as part of the Underground Railroad. If you were running from slavery, you more than likely ran to one welcoming Black community, and then another, and another. Every African American had a personal connection to slavery and the vast majority shared a universal desire for all Black people to be free. If you had a connection, then you might be able to find cooperative white people as well. This network of freedom seekers became a foundational experience for developing the African American community. Other communities have their stories to tell us as well. So New Philadelphia is unique and universal at the same time.

While we two authors remain responsible for our errors and omissions, this volume benefitted in so many ways from the collective participation of many people. First of all there are several genealogists of the McWorter family whose work has been foundational. The archival work of Thelma Elise McWorter Kirkpatrick Wheaton, who was born and raised in New Philadelphia, and the PhD dissertation and book of her daughter Juliet Walker were the starting points for most everyone. Helen McWorter Simpson of Cleveland; Karen Wall of Newton, Kansas; Lonie Wilson of Katy, Texas; and Charlotte Johnson of Alton, Illinois, assembled documents, photos, and family history books, piecing together stories. Sandra McWorter Marsh of Chicago (helped by Allen Kirkpatrick, Jr., of Chicago, now passed) gathered the collections of Ellen McWorter Yates of Kansas City, Zelia Alberta McWorter Ewing of Chicago, and Thelma McWorter Kirkpatrick Wheaton. Sandra also organized the 2005 McWorter family reunion and produced a large visual family tree. The New Philadelphia Association, led by Philip Bradshaw and a network of Pike County community leaders, volunteered in many capacities without fail. The archaeologists and historians Paul Shackel, Christopher C. Fennell, Terry Martin, Claire Martin, and Anna Agbe-Davies carried out years of research in New Philadelphia. Beginning in summer 2004, they trained more than 100 students. And as the book took shape, numerous people took the time to read and correct it, among them Larry Armistead, Phil Bradshaw, Marynel and Jerry Corton, Chris Fennell, Bennett Johnson, Charlotte King, Sandra McWorter Marsh, Terry and Claire Martin, Carol McCartney, Paul Shackel, Karen Wall, Lonie Wilson, and Harry and Helen Wright. Altogether this book relies on many people, past and present, who lived, remembered, studied, and celebrated New Philadelphia. We hope you, the reader, will celebrate with us.

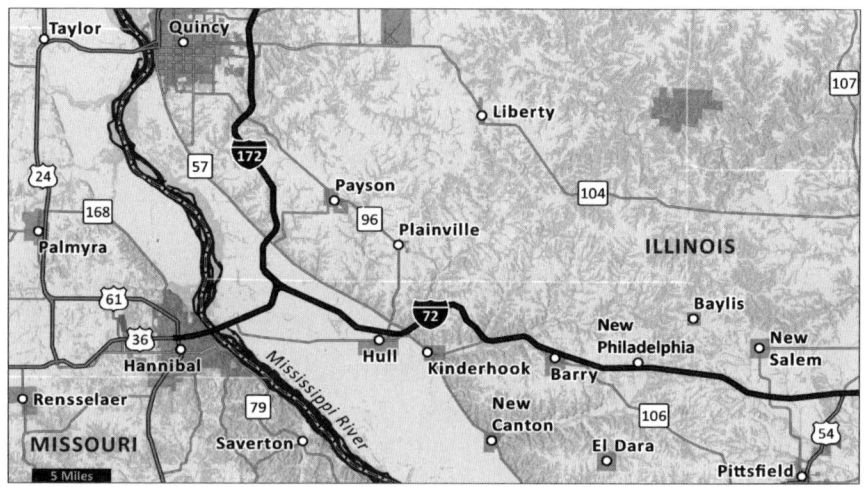

New Philadelphia and surrounding area. By James Whitacre, used with permission.

CHAPTER ONE

New Philadelphia in United States History

New Philadelphia was conceived, born, and developed as part of the United States. The U.S. itself became a country based on wars of conquest against the indigenous communities of Native Americans followed by the enslavement of Africans. First, the land was appropriated from the native peoples. Then slavery became the basis for a national economy. Until after the Civil War, slavery was central to all economic, political, and social life, both North and South. Illinois was no exception.

As for Illinois, people moved in from both North and South. Origin did not exactly mirror attitude towards slavery. Some European-American arrivals from the South are recorded as having left because they refused to be part of slavery. New York, Ohio, and Kentucky were the top three states of origin, according to the 1850 U.S. Census. But given the state's population and politics, slavery was a contentious issue and the future was uncertain.

Before the European conquests, many Native Americans lived in and around the present state of Illinois, at least 24 different peoples in multiple clans and villages. The Iroquois spread into Illinois in the late 1600s and others also found themselves pushed into Illinois from the east after battles with the European settlers. French speakers from what is now Canada were the earliest European people to arrive, and the area was claimed by France as Upper Louisiana.

The Sauk war leader Makataimeshekiakiak, also known as Black

Portrait after an 1837 oil portrait by Charles Bird King. Photo courtesy of University of Illinois at Urbana Champaign Rare Book and Manuscript Library, from McKenney and Hall, 1848. Public domain.

Hawk, fought with the British against the Americans in the War of 1812, and then in 1832 led his people in what became known as the Black Hawk War to stop the European invasion of native settlements. The battles were mostly fought in the northern part of Illinois, but Pike County and New Philadelphia were part of the contested territory.

Black Hawk wrote in his autobiography:

> For my part I am of the opinion, that so far as we have reason, we have a right to use it in determining what is right or wrong, and we should always pursue that path which we believe to be right, believing that "whatsoever is, is right." If the Great and Good Spirit wished us to believe and do as the whites, he could easily change our opinions, so that we could see, and think, and act as they do. We are nothing compared to his power, and we feel and know it....
>
> [W]herever the Great Spirit places his people they ought to be satisfied to remain, and be thankful for what He has given them, and not drive others from the country He has given them because it happens to be better than theirs. This is contrary to our way of thinking, and from my intercourse with the whites, I have learned that one great principle of *their religion* is "to do unto others as you wish them to do unto you." Those people in the mountains seem to act upon this principle, but the settlers on our frontiers and on our lands seem never to think of it, if we are to judge by their actions. (Black Hawk 1834, pages 77 and 142)

The 1830s was a decade of rapid growth in Midwestern cities and counties as settlers moved in: St. Louis went from 5,000 people to more than 16,000. Chicago grew from 350 at its founding in 1833 to 4,000 in 1840. The state capital of Springfield, Illinois, was home to 2,500 people by 1840. And Pike County grew from 2,400 in 1830 to 12,000 in 1840.

The 1830s also saw the start of the Trail of Tears, the forced removals of five Native American Nations from the Southern states to Oklahoma. These were also called death marches, because sev-

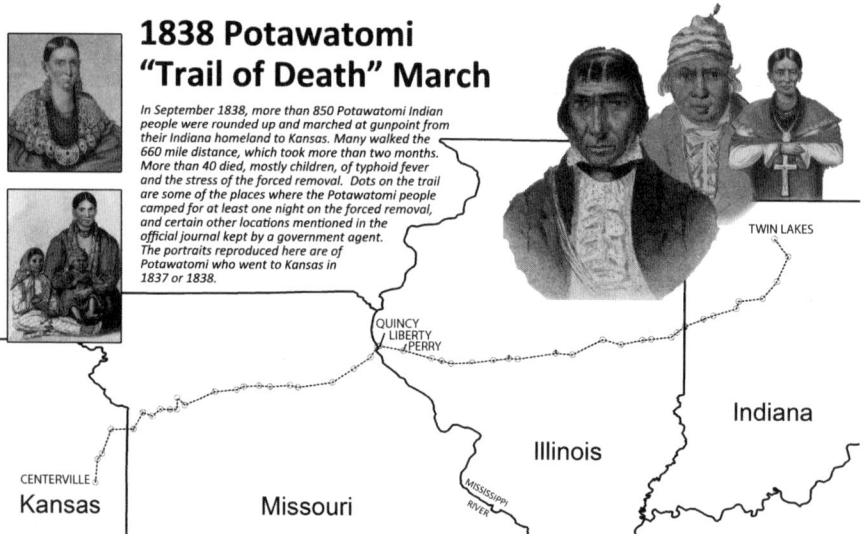

1838 Potawatomi "Trail of Death" March

In September 1838, more than 850 Potawatomi Indian people were rounded up and marched at gunpoint from their Indiana homeland to Kansas. Many walked the 660 mile distance, which took more than two months. More than 40 died, mostly children, of typhoid fever and the stress of the forced removal. Dots on the trail are some of the places where the Potawatomi people camped for at least one night on the forced removal, and certain other locations mentioned in the official journal kept by a government agent. The portraits reproduced here are of Potawatomi who went to Kansas in 1837 or 1838.

Portraits painted by George Winter of Potawatomi who were removed from Indiana to Kansas in 1837-38 shown in the map. Images reproduced from Cooke and Ramadhyani 1993. Map by Cai Yaping using data from www.potawatomi-tda.org following a design by Tom Hamilton of the Fulton County Historical Society, with permission of the society.

eral people died each day due to winter weather, lack of shoes or clothing, starvation, illness, and deadly delays. One of these marches passed through southern Illinois. But a somewhat lesser-known catastrophe was the Trail of Death, and it passed very close by New Philadelphia.

In 1838, 900 Potawatomi men, women, and children were force-marched from northern Indiana and Illinois to Kansas. The group camped 15 miles north of New Philadelphia in Liberty, Illinois. Starved and shoeless, families huddled under Mantle Rock for 20 days in December until the ferry operator at Golconda, Illinois, finally saw fit to grant them passage at an abnormally high toll fee. Crowded against the rock face but still exposed to the weather, many people died waiting. The "Indian removals" resulted from President Andrew Jackson's disregard for an 1830 Supreme Court ruling in favor of the Native Americans' legal right to stay in the Deep South. John Quincy Adams and others opposed Jackson, but he answered only to "King Cotton."

For in the early 1800s the phrase "King Cotton" defined the national economy. The nation's investment in cotton production—including owning as slaves the people who grew and harvested the crop—was greater than the entire rest of the economy. Slave owners dominated the U.S. presidency and congress. Slave-produced cotton from the United States fed the world's first industrial factories—textile mills in England and later New England. The earlier triangle trade of slaves, sugar, and rum gave way to the even more powerful triangle trade of slaves, cotton, and cloth. All this knitted the western world's economies together, centered around the Americas, Europe, and Africa.

The U.S. presidency itself reflected slavery's power. Ten of the first 12 presidents owned or had owned slaves: Washington, Jefferson, Madison, Monroe, Jackson, Van Buren, Harrison, Tyler, Polk, and Taylor. The two presidents who never owned slaves were father and son: second president John Adams and sixth president John Quincy Adams. In J. Q.'s words, slavery was "an evil of colossal magnitude." He also served in Congress and on the legal team that succeeded in defending the men who rebelled on the slave ship *Amistad*. He and 15 other signers of the 1776 Declaration of Independence never owned slaves; 41 signers did own slaves. (8th Grade American History class 2014), Two later presidents held slaves, Johnson owning many and Ulysses Grant owning and manumitting one man. It was Grant who rose to command the Union forces in the Civil War. Johnson and Grant struggled bitterly over freedom, with Grant implementing Reconstruction and protecting the Freedmen's Bureaus. How many members of Congress owned slaves has not been studied.

The state of Illinois was no exception to the power and the hunger for profit from slave production. Slavery came to the area with the first Europeans in the 1700s. Native Americans were not only enslaved but bought and sold. As Noah Lenstra described in his 2009 monograph, the notorious salt works in Gallatin County per-

The sixth U.S. President, John Quincy Adams was one of only two presidents prior to 1850 who never owned a slave, his father John Adams (the second U.S. president) being the other. Public domain. Obtained from Wikimedia Commons. Copy from 1843 by Southworth & Hawes of a lost original daguerreotype by Phillip Haas.

sisted until roughly 1850, operated by John Crenshaw (1797-1871). Besides holding slaves there to mine and extract the salt, Crenshaw also built and operated a dungeon and transfer point to enable him and others to kidnap and sell African Americans down the Mississippi River.

The Northwest Ordinance passed by Congress in 1787 prohibited slavery in the territory that would become Illinois and four other Midwestern states, but allowed residents to retain all their current property, including slaves, and spelled out that freedom seekers were to be turned over to those who had owned them. Illinois's various Black Codes set further limitations on African Americans. They could not vote, assemble in groups in public, or sue European Americans in court. In order to avoid being identified as a slave and risking kidnapping, each African American had to carry with them a certificate attesting to their freedom. While Illinois was not a slave state, early petitioners urged it to become so. The decades up to the Civil War were in a sense a race to see who would migrate in and dominate the state numerically and politically: supporters of slavery or of freedom. In the end, opinion swung to abolition, as Northerners and others wanting to farm and work as free labor dominated the state. But the road was rocky.

At the same time, Illinois was not a plantation economy. Alexis de Tocqueville draws the contrast as he saw it while traveling west down the Ohio River. He passed through some of the richest land in the country, the Old Northwest on one side and the slave states on the other:

> On the left bank of the Ohio work is connected with the idea of slavery, but on the right with well-being and progress; on the one side it is degrading, but on the other honorable; on the left bank no white laborers are to be found, for they would be afraid of being like the slaves; for work people must rely on the Negroes; but one will never see a man of leisure on the right bank: the white man's intelligent activity is used for work of every sort. (Alexis de Tocqueville, 1899, pages 345-346)

This same comparison could be made along the Mississippi River where it separated Illinois from Missouri, and in the two river towns nearest to New Philadelphia. The Mississippi River was not only the nation's primary North-South transportation route but also a boundary between slave and free territory. On the Illinois side, Quincy was located on bluffs over a network of caves. These caves hid many freedom seekers arriving from Missouri. Quincy abolitionists, many of them free African Americans, would keep watch for swimmers and climbers and escort them to a safe spot.

For example, as told by local historian Heather Bangert, one night in 1842 the free African American Barryman Barnett made contact with a freedom seeker named Charley. Barnett worked as a whitewasher, the same activity as Tom Sawyer with his white picket fence in Twain's novel. Barnett and his wife and three children lived in Quincy where he was long active on the Underground Railroad.

As he had undoubtedly done before, Barryman Barnett took Charley to Dr. Richard Eells' house in Quincy. Snatching up some dry clothes, Eells and Charley headed north in a carriage to the Mission Institute, the next safe house. Slave catchers were in hot pursuit and Charley was recaptured. On the basis of Charley's wet clothes found in the carriage, Dr. Eells was convicted of helping a fugitive.

Even after Eells passed away in 1846, other abolitionists fought his conviction all the way to the 1852 United States Supreme Court, electrifying the nation with the story of what was called "practical abolitionism." Ultimately every single court rejected his argument, but the nation was awakened as the story spread in 19th-century newspapers and rallied more to the cause of freedom. After a 20th-century campaign by Quincy activists, then-Governor Pat Quinn pardoned Richard Eells in 2014.

The National Park Service also recognized Dr. Eells' house as one of the 42 most important Underground Railroad sites nationwide. Records of the Underground Railroad, which was illegal, are scarce, but this suggests that many people did find their way to freedom with his help. It was for some time Quincy's only brick house, on a high hill above the Mississippi River, just four blocks from the

Left, The house of Dr. Richard Eells, Quincy, Illinois. Photo by Vincent L. Michael from Gutman 2015; used with permission.
Right, David Nelson, founder of the Mission Institute, Quincy, Illinois. Photo courtesy of Historical Society of Quincy and Adams County.

water, so it was highly visible.

The Mission Institute, where Dr. Eells and Charley were headed that night, was founded and run by David Nelson. It was a strongly abolitionist seminary. In 1843 proslavery vigilantes crossed the Mississippi River from Missouri and burned its chapel to the ground. But the institute continued to attract students, including at least at least two from New Philadelphia, William Shipman and his younger sister Lucretia.

If Charley had not been recaptured, he might have soon made it to the home of Congressman Owen Lovejoy in Princeton, Illinois. The farmhouse was some 50 miles northeast of Quincy and New Philadelphia. Until 1837, Owen Lovejoy worked with his brother Elijah Lovejoy in Alton in southern Illinois. That year a proslavery mob lynched Elijah and dumped his printing press into the Mississippi River. Owen then explicitly dedicated his own life to ending slavery. As he declared in a speech on the floor of Congress the first year he was elected, "Owen Lovejoy lives at Princeton, Illinois, and he aids every fugitive that comes to his door and asks it!" (Arnold 1866, page 225)

Owen Lovejoy House, Princeton, Illinois. 1905 postcard photo published by C. J. Dunbar & Co., Jewelers. Public domain.

On the Missouri side, Hannibal was 20 miles downriver from Quincy, and boasted a slave market of its own. It was also the hometown of Samuel Clemens, who grew up among his family's slaves to become the internationally known writer and abolitionist Mark Twain. When he was just a child Frank and Lucy were already farming and aiding fugitives 20 miles away across the river in Pike County, Illinois.

But not until Missouri native and now Quincy resident Terrell Dempsey researched and published *Searching for Jim* (2003) did the local history of slavery come out of the shadows in modern times. Dempsey pursued the true story behind the freedom seeker Jim in Twain's novel *Adventures of Huckleberry Finn*. As Dempsey explains in an interview with Jennifer Ciotta:

> [T]hough presently the African-American population in Hannibal is around 5 percent, yet in 1850 nearly a quarter of people here were slaves, in service to the other 75 percent. If you want to understand Mark Twain, you have to understand the world that Sam Clemens grew up in. And for any number of reasons that real story had been hidden....

Left, Samuel Clemens (1835–1910), better known as the humorist and author Mark Twain. Public domain photo by either Mathew Brady or Levin Handy in the collection of the Library of Congress.
Right, Searching for Jim by Terrell Dempsey. This book uncovered the fact that Mark Twain's father and uncle were slave traders in Hannibal. Cover image used with permission.

> I went up to the New York Historical Society and sifted through the papers of John Rogers, who was a very famous sculptor in the 19th century but lived here in Hannibal in the early 1850s and was the offspring of an abolitionist family. His letters back to the Boston area were very descriptive of the slavery that was going on here. When he decided to become a sculptor, his first sculpture was of a slave sale. Of course the only place he lived and experienced slavery was right here in Hannibal....
>
> Slavery was an integral part of Sam's boyhood. His

parents owned slaves. Sam's father was one of those guys who always moved onto the next valley because the grass was going to be greener. When John Marshall Clemens and his wife were first married, they had six slaves. They were assets thus when his business prospects shrunk, John and his wife sold the slaves. When they moved from Tennessee to Missouri in the 1830s, they only had one slave. Evidently they moved to Hannibal with that one slave, but lost him/her soon thereafter. John went broke and through a bankruptcy.

Slaves were always around the Clemens house. The family leased slaves. People do not realize this but in Missouri there was not an agricultural use for slaves. Instead they were investments. When you think of slavery in Missouri in Twain's day, you need to think of slaves as investments, as our modern day 401Ks. The way you got value out of slaves was leasing them to other people as household servants. The best way to envision how common slavery was: having a slave in the house is like having an electric dishwasher today–virtually everyone middle class or above has one. The majority of families in the county owned slaves.

Thus, the slavery that Twain was familiar with was something he whole-heartedly endorsed as a young man. Though he became a progressive thinker on race, there was nothing about slavery that bothered him as a youth. He certainly used the "n word" on occasion. Letters exist where he did that. He experienced every aspect of slavery. His father bought and sold slaves as an investment. Twain's father sued a man and got a judgment against him. Since the man did not have money, Twain's father collected his debt in the form of a nine year-old slave girl, and sold her at public auction.

At any given time there were up to a dozen slave traders in Hannibal. Twain writes at one point about a group of chained slaves who were waiting to be put on a river boat, a common site at this time. There was a smaller slave market

Jim and Huck on the Mississippi River, from the 1885 edition of The Adventures of Huckleberry Finn. *Drawing by E. W. Kemble digitized by the University of Illinois Rare Book and Manuscript Library. Public domain.*

in Hannibal, compared to New Orleans. Slaves were purchased here during Sam's time since there was a large demand for them in the cotton belt.

When you think of slavery in northeast Missouri, you have to think of it like so. At that time, there was not a banking system as we have now with federal insurance. It was risky. Therefore, slaves were a good way to pass down your estate to your children as well as a good retirement tool. Slaves multiplied. Once a year your female slaves would reproduce thus increasing the value of your portfolio. Then you

> would lease them out year to year, the contract lasting from Christmas Day to Christmas Day. The person who rented the slave agreed to provide a change or two of clothing, a pair of shoes and agreed to pay for any doctor visits that were necessary–all for $25. This was the world that Twain grew up in.
>
> Sam also wrote about having to eat and sleep with the slaves. There was a myth that there were slave quarters everywhere, but they actually generally slept on pallets on the floor, in the kitchen or in an out building or basement. When you think of living arrangements for slaves, without sounding demeaning, think of how a dog sleeps. They were expected to sleep on the floor, out of the way. They had to be the first ones up to start the fire, empty the night chambers, etc.

Twain did not admit any of this publicly, in effect sanitizing his family history. But his writing and speeches (which came after the Civil War) served to awaken and galvanize a worldwide readership to injustices both here and abroad, in particular his novel *Adventures of Huckleberry Finn*. In this novel, one of the heroes, Jim, is fleeing slavery, aiming for Cairo, Illinois, where he plans to buy his family out of slavery. Huckleberry Finn has joined him and Huck's friend Tom Sawyer helps, too. Even though Twain's work was plagued by stereotypes and prejudices, his voice became a literary cry against slavery.

De Tocqueville's two-volume *Democracy in America* is one of the most cited studies on the early development of the United States. He was a French aristocrat who traveled through the eastern states and the Midwest in 1831 to investigate the North American experiment in a new political system. He was positively impressed, writing in one passage:

> Town meetings are to liberty what primary schools are to science; they bring it within the people's reach, they teach men how to use and enjoy it. (de Tocqueville 1899, page 60)

What is less cited is that he also expressed some skepticism, for instance:

> There is no country in the world in which everything can be provided for by laws, or in which political institutions can

Painting of Alexis de Tocqueville by Théodore Chassériau. From the collection of the Chateau de Versailles. From Wikimedia Commons.

prove a substitute for common sense and public morality. (de Tocqueville 1899, page 120)

But still less known by far is the fact that de Tocqueville traveled with a colleague who became his lifelong friend. This was Gustave de Beaumont, and he wrote a novel presenting his own impressions of the United States. *Marie, or, Slavery in the United States*, was widely read in France in the 1800s but not published in English until 1958. The novel paints a portrait of racism against African Americans and Native Americans that is an undeniable counterweight to the democracy that de Tocqueville celebrates. For instance:

The misery of the black people oppressed by American soci-

> ety cannot be compared with that of any of the unfortunate classes among other peoples. Everywhere there exists hostility between the rich and the proletariat; however, the two classes are not separated by any insurmountable barrier: the poor become rich, the rich poor; that is enough to temper the oppression of the one by the other. But when the American crushes the black population with such contempt, he knows that he need never fear to experience the fate reserved for the Negro. I was continually witnessing some sad happening which revealed to me the profound hatred of the Americans for the blacks. (de Beaumont 1958, page 74)

The mid-19th century was a time of a great moral and legal opposition to slavery that led to the bloody military confrontation of the Civil War. Many people joined this opposition; two voices are especially striking, the African American Harriet Tubman and the European American Abby Kelley. Harriet Tubman wrote, "I had reasoned this out in my mind, there was one of two things I had a right to, liberty or death; if I could not have one, I would have the other." (Bradford 1886, page 29) Abby Kelley echoed this from where she stood: "I rejoice to be identified with the despised people of color. If they are to be despised, so ought their advocates to be." (Sterling 1991, page 86).

Abraham Lincoln (1809–1865), who as president during the Civil War would be central to the struggle over slavery, came to Illinois at the age of 21 and entered politics in that state. In 1816 he had migrated with his family from Kentucky to Indiana. The family then moved to Illinois in 1830. In 1831 Lincoln set off on his own for New Salem in Sangamon County. He fought in the Black Hawk War, began studying law on his own, and was elected to the Illinois Legislature. Moving to the state capital of Springfield, he passed the bar exam and began to practice law all over west-central Illinois.

Lincoln set his sights on becoming U.S. Senator from Illinois, running against the incumbent, Stephen Douglas, in the 1858 election. He challenged Douglas to seven debates, which took place in different cities across the state. One of the final debates was on October 13,

Etching of Gustave de Beaumont by an unknown artist. From Assemblée Nationale: Galerie des Representants du Peuple, *1848. Courtesy of the Beinecke Rare Book and Manuscript Library, Yale University. Digital file retrieved from Wikimedia. Public domain.*

1858 in Quincy, 30 miles north of New Philadelphia. In each debate the topic was slavery, Lincoln speaking against it in what was a divided state and nation. Douglas won re-election as senator, but the two engaged in such extended and skilled rhetoric on the topic of slavery that the texts of the debates, printed and reprinted, helped propel Lincoln into the presidency just two years later. However, Lerone Bennett (2000) has shown that Lincoln was a consummate politician who was forced to end slavery by the actions of both the abolitionist movement and the slaveholding states. And at its base, that movement was powered by the actions of slaves, former slaves, and their allies.

In the territory of Illinois, slavery was legal; that ended in 1818 with statehood and a state constitution. But then the Illinois "Black laws" placed Black people in slave-like conditions until the Civil War in 1861. Black laws set severe limits on the democratic rights of African Americans. Black people could not assemble in groups in public, bear arms, or bring legal suits against white people in court. They

Top left, Illinois State Senator Abraham Lincoln in 1858. Ambrotype by Abraham Byers of Beardstown, Illinois. Ostendorf #O-5. 7 May 1858. Digital image from Daniel W. Stowell. From Wikimedia. Public domain. *Top right,* Forced into Glory: Abraham Lincoln's White Dream *by Lerone Bennett. Cover image used with permission of Lerone Bennett.* *Bottom,* United States postage stamp commemorating the debates between Lincoln and Douglas. iStock photo by Mike Rega, used with permission.

had to carry certificates of freedom to avoid being considered slaves and carried off into a slave state.

These laws were hotly debated and fought over in encounters all over Illinois. Sometimes people got free. Sometimes the slave catch-

The Discovery of Nat Turner.

Nat Turner's capture. This image was reproduced frequently, testifying to the centrality of the slavery debate in the United States. Public domain image from Andrews 1895; digitized by the University of Illinois at Urbana Champaign Rare Books and Manuscripts Library.

ers and slave owners won. Across the Mississippi River in the Civil War border state of Missouri, slavery existed until 1865, two years after the Emancipation Proclamation freed slaves in the Southern states "in rebellion." A Missouri state convention and an executive order by then-Governor Thomas C. Fletcher ended it.

Mural by Hale Woodruff (1900–1980) showing the defiance of the Amistad rebels during their trial in 1838. Image used with permission of Talladega College.

Today the towns and farms between Hannibal, Missouri, to the west, Springfield, Illinois, to the east, Quincy to the north, and Alton to the south are historical landmarks of abolitionism as practiced by European descendants. But the story of New Philadelphia introduces some of the many African Americans who were also active for their own freedom, who made their own contributions to the democratic transformation of the country.

The self-determination of African Americans (among others) has been marginalized or omitted from the narrative of the nation's history, although it has forced its way into the public consciousness throughout that history. Africans resisted by fighting back against all aspects of slavery: to begin with, they made the case against it in speeches and publications that sparked debate and shaped opinion. Sometimes the fight was with guns, e.g., Nat Turner's 1831 rebellion, one of the few events that still lives in the popular imagination.

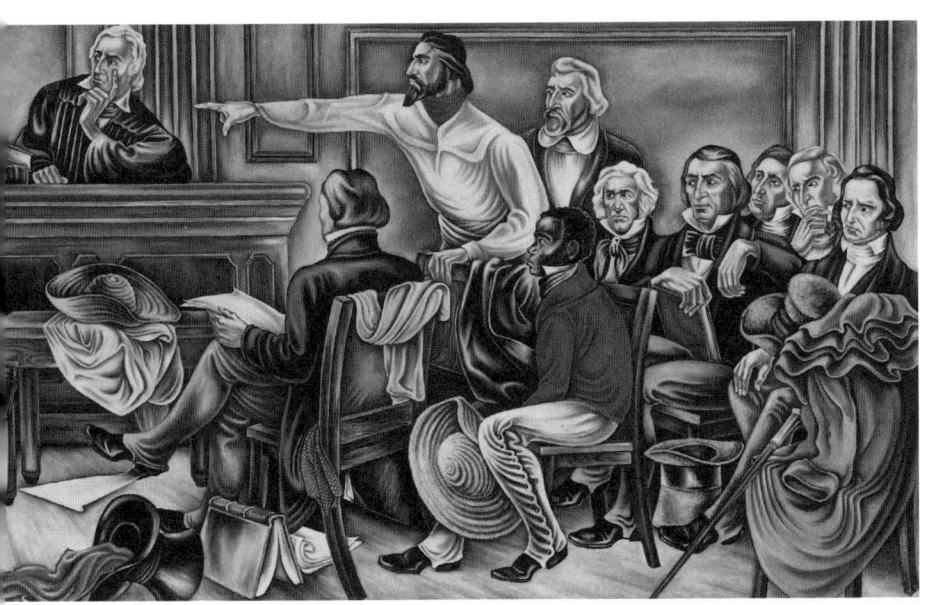

Following the Greek saying that desperate times call for desperate measures, Nat is a hero, to African Americans in particular. Other times it was with singing and dancing to affirm an identity that resisted the designs of the oppressors. All this began in the slave castles on the coast of West Africa, and continued on the slave ship, such as the 1839 rebellion aboard the *Amistad*. Newspapers on both sides of the Atlantic Ocean followed the trial of the rebels, exciting and informing people regarding the question of liberty for the slave. This resistance became a definitive feature of the plantation system, and was commemorated down through the generations. Hale Woodruff was an Illinois-born African American muralist, painter, and printmaker who took up many themes of heritage and history and portrayed the *Amistad* rebellion in three of his six famous Talladega murals.

New Philadelphia is an expression of this self-determination in both spirit and purpose. As the first town founded by an African American, it is an iconic symbol of how Black people were active participants in inventing the country. New Philadelphia was an act of freedom-making against all odds, almost entirely surrounded by proslavery forces.

Bust of Free Frank McWorter, 1777—1854, founder of New Philadelphia, by great-great-granddaughter, Shirley McWorter Moss. Photo courtesy of the Abraham Lincoln Presidential Library & Museum.

Chapter Two

Founding Family

The family that founded New Philadelphia had its own founders: Free Frank, or as he was later known, Frank McWorter, and Free Lucy, later Lucy Denham, finally Lucy McWorter. Frank was born in 1777 in South Carolina. His mother Juda had made the terrible crossing from West Africa after being kidnapped or sold to slave traders. His father George McWorter held his mother in slavery. As Nina Simone wrote and sang, "My father was rich and white/He forced my mother late one night." Family oral history tells that Juda ran to the woods to give birth to their son and then presented the newborn to George, thus preventing George's wife from harming her or the baby. So like many slaveholders, George owned his son—and he never freed him.

History records Frank as a "yellow man" who could neither read nor write. But he is also recorded as a remarkable and bold man. He liberated his wife, children, and grandchildren at a time when family members were too often sold, taken to distant states, and lost forever. He helped so many others find freedom too. Frank only was able to accomplish this because freedom became his family's mission too. The bronze bust shown here is the work of his great-great-granddaughter Shirley McWorter Moss. With no existing image of Frank, Shirley examined family photographs and studied the faces of living male descendants and "added and subtracted," as she puts it, to arrive at Frank's own appearance. Her creative impulse was guided by family stories of freedom and self-reliance.

Free Frank, resident in Pulaski County, Kentucky, might have gotten his name because in 1819 at the age of 42 he had finally earned enough funds to purchase his own freedom. But it could also have been because of his lifelong dedication to freedom. He and his family fought for freedom in seven ways: They ran. They bought family members out of slavery. They worked and traded their way. They helped others run. They founded a town named Philadelphia—City of Brotherly Love—which was a signal to others. They fought in the Civil War. And they lived free on their own land, with guns, 20 miles from slavery.

The success of the McWorters' freedom mission relied on relentless work by everyone involved—caring for each other, growing and raising crops and animals, and buying and selling natural resources, including the land itself. This ethic survives today among McWorter descendants and Pike County locals alike. The 20th-century freedom seeker Hollis Watkins, speaking from rural Mississippi, describes the tradition as he lived it:

> As long as I've been conscious about being alive, I've been a worker. I can't remember a time that I've never worked. Work wasn't just a rite of passage; it was one of the primary aspects of life that allowed a person to be a part of the family and community. Work allowed anyone to earn one's way into the tribe. Yes, as a baby, one is loved unconditionally by the tribe. But, before a child is taught much else, one learns that work or being a good worker is fundamental to being a good family and community member because one was contributing to the survival and progress of the whole group. (Watkins 2015, page 11)

When Frank was 19, his father George took him along to some land he had come to own in Kentucky. Frank's great grandson Arthur attributed this move to the fact that he was so closely related to George's white children. (Walker 1983, page 7) Several of these children were very close to Frank's age, according to Alan D. McWhirter writing on a website devoted to McWh*rter genealogy.

George set Frank to clearing the land for cultivation. Frank was a hard worker and grew into managing the Kentucky farm, even while a slave. While he also put Frank in a position to manage the

"Free Lucy" McWorter (1771–1870). Lucy outlived her husband by 16 years and provided leadership for her family along with her son Solomon. She gave birth to at least 17 children, 7 of whom survived. Photo used with permission of the family; from the New Philadelphia Collection found in Newton, Kansas by descendant Conle White, great-grandson of Hiley McWorter Clark.

farm, he never freed him.

But Frank met a woman named Lucy living on the nearby Denham plantation. Lucy was six years older than him. In 1799 the two of them committed to each other. No legal marriage was possible and they were still owned by different people, but they began to have children. Over the years she became known as Free Lucy, which suggests something about her identity as well and begins to compensate for the near lack of further details about her. But one thing is clear: the family's achievements rested not only on hard work but also on a solid life partnership between Frank and Lucy. They actually married twice, with the second time being on March 9, 1839 when they were both free in Illinois.

What helped get the McWorters started on this freedom mission is that when barely out of his teens, Frank was able to harness an important natural resource: niter. During Frank's time, in Kentucky's now-famous Mammoth Cave, slaves were driven to break the niter-rich rock from the cave walls and carry it outside for processing into saltpeter. Working smaller caves in that same area, Frank was able to mine and manufacture his own saltpeter. Saltpeter, sulfur, and charcoal together make the explosive called gunpowder.

When the War of 1812 began, Frank was able to sell even more saltpeter, and for a good profit. More than the profit, there was another aspect of this important for Frank's development. By helping arm the American army, Frank was empowering himself, and the centrality of gunpowder in this effort to end British colonization gave him a glimpse of what might be possible and necessary to gain freedom. He didn't know it, but he was setting a precedent for his grandsons fighting in the Civil War 50 years later.

Frank's own path to freedom was based very much on his entrepreneurial success and diplomatic skill. He purchased his family out of slavery. He and Lucy were committed to each other. They already had four children, all born into slavery: Juda, Frank, Jr,. Sarah, and Solomon. Frank began saving money so he could change all of this. His first purchase, made in 1817, was critical. He bought his wife, who was 46 years old, out of slavery, and she was pregnant. Thus their fifth child, Squire, was born free.

The official deed book of the county includes the following record concerning Lucy. It became her freedom paper:

> Know all men by these presents that I William Dunham being desirous for certain reasons to liberate from a state of slavery my Negro woman Lucy, a yellow or Mutatto [sic] woman.... I William Dunham in pursuance to an act of the general assembly of the Commonwealth of Kentucky authorizing the owner of slaves by their last will and testament or by any other instrument of writing ... by these presents emancipate And set free my said Negro woman Lucy from my service as a slave ... set my hand and seal this 7th day of

> April 1817. Wit Jon Porter, Joshua Jones, Aaron Sargent (From the recorded deeds of Pulaski County, Kentucky, volume 3 page 228. Text courtesy of http://kykinfolk.org/pulaski/poc/trans.html)

Two years later, in 1819, he was able to buy his own freedom. The deed book contains this text, which became Frank's freedom paper:

> Know all men by these presents that I Abner McWhorter of the county of Lincoln and the state of Tennessee and one of the heirs of George McWhorter dec. late of said county aforesaid for myself and also Attorney in fact for the rest of the heirs and representatives of said George McWhorter dec. to wit: John McWhorter, Adam Morris & Amos Morris, being desirous and willing on our part (It being to our knowledge the will and desire of our late father & father in law) to liberate from a state of slavery a certain Negro man named Frank a yellow man.
>
> I the said Abner McWhorter being at this time in the County of Pulaski & State of Kentucky where said Negro man Frank does and has been suffered to reside for [?] years previous to the death of my said father and being authorized by the rest of the heirs ... do therefore hereby free said Negro man agreeable to the laws of the state of Kentucky.... seals this 13th day of September 1819. Wit. Aaron Sargent, David Cooper, Joshua Jones, William Bath (From the recorded deeds of Pulaski County, Kentucky, volume 4 page 136. Text courtesy of http://kykinfolk.org/pulaski/poc/trans.html)

Other documents spell out that Frank's liberation was accomplished by him purchasing himself for $800—the equivalent of $15,000 today—even though Frank's first owner was his own father and his final owner also a relative.

But as the global markets for sugar and cotton and other slave-produced commodities expanded, so did the institution of slavery. Kentucky became more hostile to free Black people and slavery became more permanent and, if it was possible, harsh. In 1826

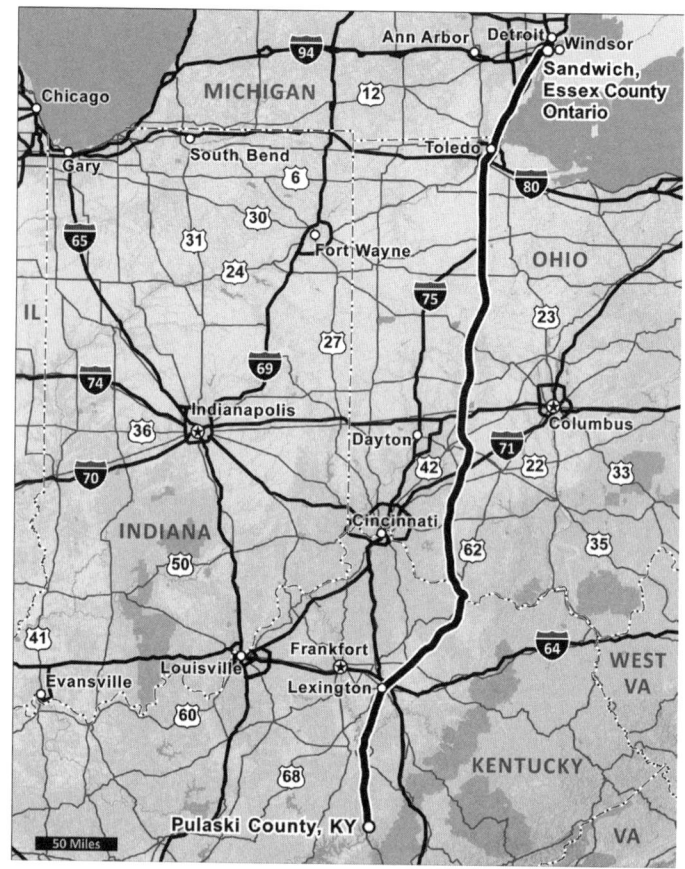

The route Frank, Jr took in 1826 from Pulaski County, KY to Essex County, ON, Canada was 420 miles long and included stops at several known Underground Railroad sites. Map by James Whitacre, used with permission.

Frank, Jr ran on the Underground Railroad to Canada, where he was eventually able to buy land and find a wife.

As with almost every freedom seeker, the dramatic details of Frank, Jr's flight are not known, but it was bound up with the family's arrival in Pike County. Once free in Canada, Frank, Jr. received mail in Sandwich, Essex County, which was a long-renowned African-Canadian and abolitionist community just across the river from Detroit, in what is now Windsor, Ontario. There he married an English woman named Mary Ann. It is likely that he and his wife

First part of 1841 letter to Frank McWorter, Jr. in Sandwich, Ontario. Image from the McWorter family courtesy of Allen Kirkpatrick, Jr.

worshipped as part of what became Sandwich First Baptist Church with his fellow former slaves. The congregation made bricks for and built this church; it was designed with tunnels and a trapdoor to hide the many fugitive congregants when the pastor sang out particular hymns as cue to action. An 1843 legal document signed with an X by Frank, Jr. details his sale of 50 acres of a 100-acre parcel of land to a Peter Hollinworth and gives Frank, Jr.'s address as Talbot Middle Road, Rochester Township, Essex County, Western District, Canada.

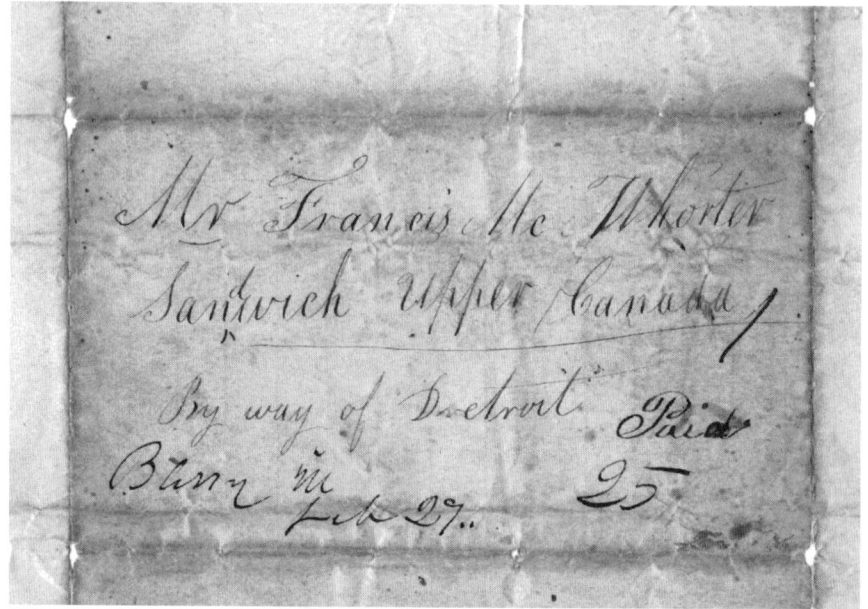

Top, *Another letter addressed to Frank McWorter with the Sandwich address. Photo from the McWorter family courtesy of Allen Kirkpatrick, Jr.* **Bottom**, *Sandwich Church, Windsor, Ontario. Photo courtesy of Reynolds Farley and Judy Mullin, Detroit1707.org.*

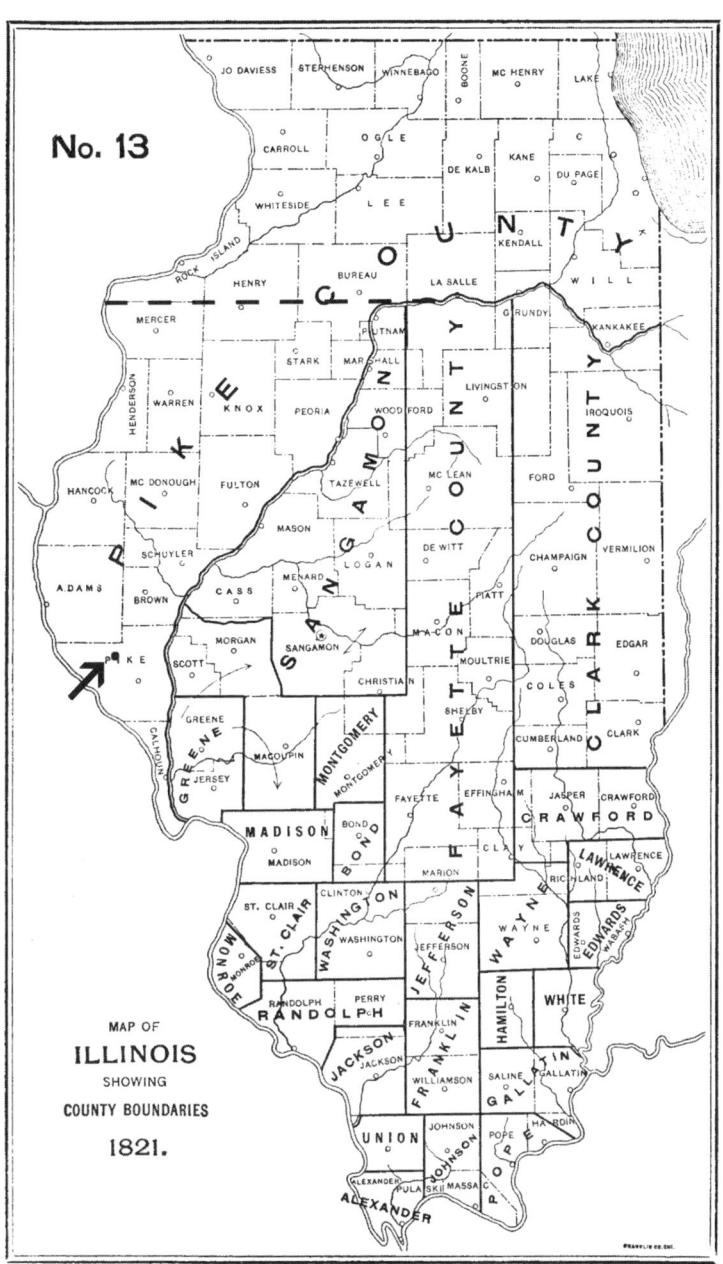

Frank McWorter's land purchase in Illinois is indicated by the dot and arrow on this map. In 1821 Pike County was much larger than today, reaching all the way north to Lake Michigan. Pike County land below the dotted line was the Illinois Military Tract. Map from Rose 1906, page 41. Marks added.

McWorter descendant and historian Juliet Walker explains what happened next. After being turned down many times by his son's former owner, Frank the father was finally able to trade his saltpeter mining and extracting operation for freedom for Frank the son. He had to pay the premium that was demanded for a slave who had run away. He then arranged for his son's freedom papers to be delivered to him 400 miles away in Canada. That way Frank, Jr could travel back to Kentucky. For with the pressures on free black Kentuckians rising, the McWorters were making ready to leave the slave state, and Frank, Jr. was critical to that journey.

Soon after purchasing his son's freedom, Frank the father bought land in the Illinois Military Tract, sight unseen. This land (and military tracts elsewhere) were granted to veterans of the War of 1812, 160 acres per person as partial payment for their military service. Most sold their acres, and several decades of land speculation, squatting, sales, and ultimately settlement followed. Dr. Elliot, who sold him the Pike County land, had not seen it either. To be sure the land was good, Juliet Walker relates that Frank first arranged for someone else traveling that way to examine it and report back. Joseph Porter, later a justice of the peace in Kentucky, brought word to Frank that the land was situated in rolling terrain, high ground, a mix of prairie and forest, and with fresh flowing water. To pay for the Illinois land, Frank sold the rest of the Kentucky farm that he had created out of the wilderness.

Another crucial step was to obtain a character reference signed by 19 Kentucky neighbors, starting with the same Joseph Porter. This document was part of making a safe passage and being able to settle in Illinois. Another part was a bond payment due from any free black moving to the state, and Frank could satisfy that requirement by showing ownership of Illinois land. And so he bought the Illinois acreage.

With all these and more preparations made, in 1830 six members of the McWorter family left Kentucky for a free life in Illinois: Frank, age 53; Lucy, 59; Frank, Jr., 26; Squire, 13; Commodore, 7; and Lucy Ann, 5. More resources would be needed to come back for

Juda, age 30; Sarah, 19; Solomon, 15; and at least one grandchild, Charlotte, age 4. We can only imagine how tough the family separation was. But a plan was in place that would free them all.

In sum, the preparing to move to Illinois and freedom for the first free McWorters spanned two years and included these steps, as explained in Walker (1983):

- **December 1828:** Frank sold 59 acres in Kentucky for $105.50
- **May 1829:** He traded the saltpeter enterprise for Frank, Jr.'s freedom
- **September 7, 1830:** Nineteen people in Pulaski County, Kentucky, sign a character reference for Frank
- **September 13, 1830:** Frank bought Illinois land for $200.00
- **September 15:** He sold a 50-acre tract of land in Kentucky

The journey west was arduous in many ways. The distance was some 500 miles, which could take three months without storms, bitter cold, or other hazards. In 1830 it was familiar to Native Americans, but mostly wilderness to settlers, including the McWorters. Illinois was the most challenging land to cross, in part because winter arrived just when they did.

The noted abolitionist Levi Coffin of Ohio wrote of his travel to Illinois in some detail. He was the European American known as the President of the Underground Railroad for his tireless aid to freedom seekers and his advocacy of "practical abolition." Coffin himself wrote of turning back in defeat trying to cross Illinois. After losing his way, he ran out of food. Swarms of mosquitoes attacked him more than once. When Coffin found other settlers near Springfield, Illinois, as he writes,

> Words can not express the thankfulness that filled my heart; I was gladder to see these people than I had ever been to see my nearest friends. No one can realize our feelings who has not had a similar experience. The people welcomed us to their cabin and soon prepared for us an excellent dinner of fresh venison, warm corn-bread, wild honey, milk and butter. They told us that three families, their own and two others, had settled in that locality the year before, and had raised a

very good crop in the summer, It was twenty-five miles to their nearest neighbors, near the forks of the river. (Coffin 1880, page 93)

Coffin pressed westward to his destination, his sister-in-law's pioneer homestead near present-day Peoria, only to face one more challenge: desperately managing to save his horse in a raging stream. Another traveler soon gave him encouraging advice. But in Coffin's own words, "I told them that ever since I had come to the West I had heard of a better place a little farther on, and now that I had got within forty miles of it, I thought I would turn back." He reversed course east back to Ohio. His sister-in-law's family recorded this account of difficulties on their migration journey from Ohio just a few years earlier:

> Although we were well outfitted with good horses and wagons, many hardships awaited us of which we had not dreamed. We had a terrible trip through Indiana through mud, over logs and brush, often swamped down to the hubs of the wagon. We could procure but little feed for our horses but new corn, and part of the time could not obtain that; and when at last we struck the Grand Prairie, west of Clinton, on the Wabash, we found ourselves with broken-down horses and only three days' provisions…. The country before us was wild, new, almost untrodden by man; but our hearts were brave….
>
> The next day we reached our destination [in Sangamon County, Illinois]. We were among strangers, but they were kind, generous and hospitable. Winter was drawing near, and we had no shelter of any kind in which to stay, no feed for our stock, and my wife the only person among us who had not been sick on the road, and yet we succeeded in passing our first winter in Illinois, as best we could, and without losing much stock….
>
> The summer following much sickness prevailed, and in the fall we lost two children, which discouraged us very much,—made us home-sick, and almost induced us to return

to Ohio. (Nathan Dillon quoted in *History of Tazewell County, Illinois....* 1879, pages 201-202)

Coffin and the Dillon family could travel and meet other settlers as equals on roads and trails. The McWorters had to have their freedom papers at the ready to show anyone they met. They also had to have loaded guns ready to show those who were not respectful of paper. This on top of being ready to negotiate passage with Native Americans who might not speak or read English. And unlike Coffin, who had inherited some wealth from his and his wife's families, the McWorters had only their own savings, depleted by the high cost of their own persons.

And so three adult McWorters and three children left Kentucky in 1830, but were forced to spend the winter of 1830-31 in nearby Greene County, Illinois. For along with the challenges of economics, racist terror, and disease, they met the challenge of a very tough winter. Abraham Lincoln and his family were also stranded in their migration to Illinois that same season. Here is a report that includes quotes from Dr. Julian M. Sturtevant, who was then helping start Illinois College in nearby Jacksonville, Illinois:

> The Winter of Deep Snow blanketed southern Illinois and perhaps the entire state to a depth of three feet on the level, drifts of four to six feet. Storms with high winds continued for 60 days; many families were snowbound in their homes and travelers remained wherever they happened to be when the heavy snow started....
>
> A cold rain started December 20, 1830 occasionally changing to sleet or snow until the day before Christmas, when large soft flakes fell to a depth of six inches. This was followed by a furious gale and a driving snow that piled up to three feet. Then came a rain that froze as it fell, forming a crust, "Nearly, but not quite, strong enough to bear a man" and over this a few inches of light snow. John Buckles described this icy crust in Logan County as "Strong enough to bear the weight of team and sled."
>
> "The clouds passed away and the wind came down

> from the northwest with extraordinary ferocity," says Sturtevant. "For weeks, certainly for not less than two weeks, the mercury in the thermometer tube was not, on any one morning, higher than 12 degrees below zero. The wind was a steady, fierce gale from the northwest, day and night. The air was filled with flying snow, which blinded the eyes and almost stopped the breath of anyone who attempted to face it. No man could, for any considerable length of time, make his way on foot against it....
>
> Herds of buffalo also floundered in the deep snow and starved. It has been said that the Winter of the Deep Snow took the last of the buffalo from east of the Mississippi River. ("Winter of the Deep Snow" 1968, pages 1 and 3.)

All this was a real test of McWorter family unity and resourcefulness as they faced the challenge of housing and feeding themselves and the livestock they brought and protecting their almost irreplaceable tools. But they survived. As the land thawed and the landscape once again turned green, they made the final leg of the journey. The Native Americans had been driven out, and no other settlers had yet arrived to settle in Pike County's Hadley Township.

As the excerpts here suggest, the historical record is very one-sided. Accounts of the geography and the physical hardships are available. Tales told by settlers of their encounters with Native Americans are published, perhaps most famously by the children's author Laura Ingalls Wilder, but hardly any stories by Native Americans have been published. Accounts of the special hardships facing freedom seekers in this period are also scarce. There are two reasons for this. First, the freedom seekers often could not write, because it was illegal to teach a slave to read or write. If it was known that you could, any slave owner might well take it out on you. Second, slaves and even free Black people had less of the privilege of free time to write or tell their accounts, because they were not resting on multiple generations of wealth building. Another way to put this is that African Americans are in many ways still running. On the run, you don't often put pen to paper.

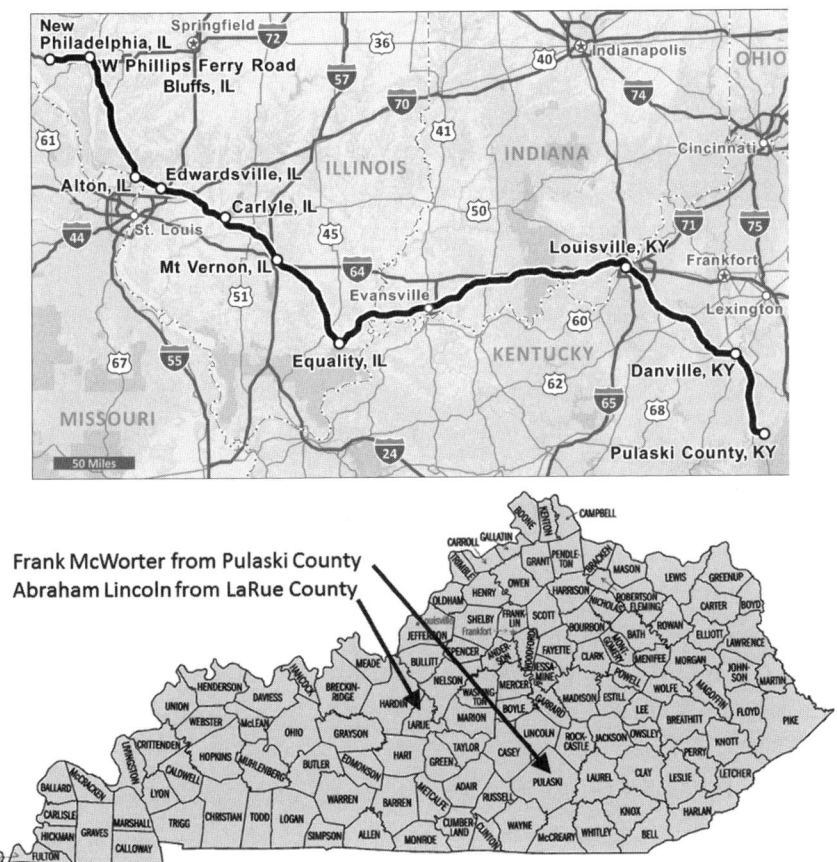

Top, The route shown here passes through places named by Juliet Walker in her account of the McWorters' journey to Illinois. Map by James Whitacre; used with permission.
Bottom, Frank McWorter and his family were held in slavery in Pulaski County, Kentucky; Abraham Lincoln lived just two counties away in LaRue County. Map courtesy of Wikipedia.org; details added by authors.

It was three years before any additional settlers arrived in Hadley Township. The closest people when the McWorter family arrived were European Americans, the Blair family in particular, living in the vicinity of what would become Worcester, later renamed Barry, five miles west. Frank and Lucy McWorter soon joined the Baptist Church, founded 1829 in the vicinity of New Canton and later moved to Barry.

The first task in 1831 was to secure the family and provide for survival in the new territory. On that basis the family's life work could proceed: Freeing the rest of the family and everyone else they could. Averaging 20 miles per day, the one-way trip might take one month. This involved the cost of travel as well as the purchase of a relative, so building and maintaining a freedom budget was a serious undertaking. Furthermore, Kentucky had begun to curtail the buying and importing of slaves, but slavery was in full swing and many cities were witness to murderous riots against Black people and abolitionists. Frank made three trips to buy three of his children: Solomon in 1835 at age 20 (Frank's last child born into slavery), Sarah in 1843 at age 32, and Juda in 1850 at age 50. Sons were freed before daughters, most likely in order to provide security for the others who would come, and the sons died younger. The tough decisions of whom to free next would have been guided first of all by questions of safety and survival, in both Kentucky and Illinois. Between 1817 and 1857 the McWorters purchased 16 family members out of slavery for a total of about $14,000. This is equal to nearly $500,000 in 2015 dollars.

The Pulaski County (Kentucky) court record that became Solomon's freedom paper reads as follows:

> Be it known to all whom it may concern, that whereas the undersigned Free Frank of Pike Co of the state of Illinois have purchased a mulatto boy named Solomon aged about twenty one years (a slave purchased from John Eastham Sr of the state of Pulaski and state of Kentucky for the sum of five hundred and fifty dollars, and for diverse considerations have determined to emancipate and set free the said Solomon. Therefore, by these presents emancipate him from all obligations to me or my heirs ... I the said free Frank hereunto set my name and seal this 7th day of August 1835. Acknowledged by Free Frank in open court 17 August 1835. William Fox, Clerk (From the recorded deeds of Pulaski County, Kentucky, volume 8 page 199. Text courtesy of http://kykinfolk.org/pulaski/poc/trans.html)

> AN ACT to change the name of Free Frank.   In force 19th Jan, 1837
>
> Sec. 1. Be it enacted by the people of the State of Illinois represented in the General Assembly, That the name of Free Frank, of the county of Pike and State of Illinois, be and is hereby changed to that of Frank McWorter, by which latter name he shall hereafter be called and known, and sue and be sued, plead and be impleaded, purchase and convey both real and personal property in said last mentioned name, and the children of said Free Frank shall hereafter take the name of their father, as changed and provided for by this act.
>
> Sec. 2. This act to be in force from and after its passage.
>
> Approved 19th January, 1837.

Name changed to Frank McWortle

Powers, &c.

Full text of McWorter Law. From Laws of the State of Illinois... 1837. *Public domain.*

As an African American, a landowner and someone in the process of establishing a town, Free Frank needed to affirm his legal status as a citizen. Free Frank legally became Frank McWorter and secured his rights as a citizen by obtaining passage of the McWorter Law. A reminiscence published very recently offers a window into local attitudes and actions:

> [S]ome local people did support Free Frank and his family. Among these were William Ross and Abraham Scholl. Ross, influential in the county's beginning, helped Free Frank acquire legal rights to his property, and (when Ross was a state senator) "presented Free Frank's name-changing petition to the Illinois General Assembly." Free Frank took as his surname McWorter, which was a variation of the spelling of his original slave owner, George McWhorter. Scholl, who lived nearby in Pike County, and was known to dislike slavery, was said to take a "kindly interest in the old man [Free Frank] and his struggle to free his family from the galling yoke of southern slavery. (Payne 2011, page 268)

The McWorter Law passed on January 19, 1837. The *Lincoln Log*,

Top, March 9, 1839 certificate of Frank and Lucy McWorter's marriage. Document courtesy of Karen Wall.
Bottom, An 1829–1860 minute book of the Barry Baptist Church, four miles west of New Philadelphia. Photo courtesy of Barry Baptist Church.

The original text of two Barry Baptist Church decisions recorded on Saturday, May 4, 1833. Photo courtesy of Barry Baptist Church.

a day-by-day account of Abraham Lincoln's life, and the *1836 [-1837] Journal of the House of Representatives of the General Assembly of the State of Illinois* both document Lincoln as present and active in the state legislature on that day when it convened in Vandalia, Illinois. This is the only existing documentation of Frank and Abe crossing paths; but in that sparsely populated central Illinois of the early-to-mid-1800s, it is quite likely that they at least knew of each other.

Not even two months after Frank was legally recognized as Frank McWorter, he and Lucy got married as free residents of Illinois. When Frank was asked if he would live with, cherish, and support his wife, he answered, "Why, God bless your soul, I've been doing that very thing for the past forty years!"

The early pages of the Barry Baptist Church minutes include these texts: first, "the church agree to Send a letter and messengers to meet a convention of the Sister churches at blue river on the 2nd Saturday in June next to arrange an association," and second, "agree that the clerk write a letter for inspection tomorrow and that brother Martin Wm Freeman and Bro free frank bear it." So just two years after his arrival to Illinois, Frank is designated along with two others to represent his church at a meeting to help form an association. It is quite likely that the church was also facilitating freedom work in the county. According to Janita Metcalf, curator of the Barry Historical Museum until her death in 2014, the Blue River Church stood on Blue River between Pittsfield and Detroit, Illinois, about 20 miles from New Philadelphia.

	Relation	Lifespan	Year freed	Age freed	Years lived free
Frank	father	1777-1854, 77 years	1819	42	35
Lucy	mother	1771-1870, 99 years	1817	46	52
Juda	daughter	1800-1906, 106 years	1850	50	56
Frank, Jr.	son	1804-1851, 47 years	1829?	25	22
Sarah (Sally)	daughter	1811-1891, 80 years	1843	32	48
Solomon	son	1815-1879, 64 years	1835	20	44
Squire	son	1817-1855, 38 years	--	born free	38
Commodore	son	1823-1855, 32 years	--	born free	32
Lucy Ann	daughter	1825-1902, 77 years	--	born free	77

Top, Map showing land ownership around New Philadelphia as of 1872. From Ensign 1872, page 100.

Bottom, Dates of birth, freedom, and death for each person in the first and second generations of the Frank McWorter family. Data from Walker 1983.

As McWorter friend and neighbor Clarissa Shipman wrote in 1840, "The Baptists have a meeting once a month in Worchester [later renamed Barry] they have a very good preacher he is an Eastern man I always attend when I can." (Letter in the collection of the Winterthur Museum, Garden and Library.) Frank, Lucy, and their son Commodore were listed as Barry Baptist Church members through the 1840s and mid-1850s. A note in the minutes book 21 years later reads: "Bro Frank McWorter died Sept 7th 1854."

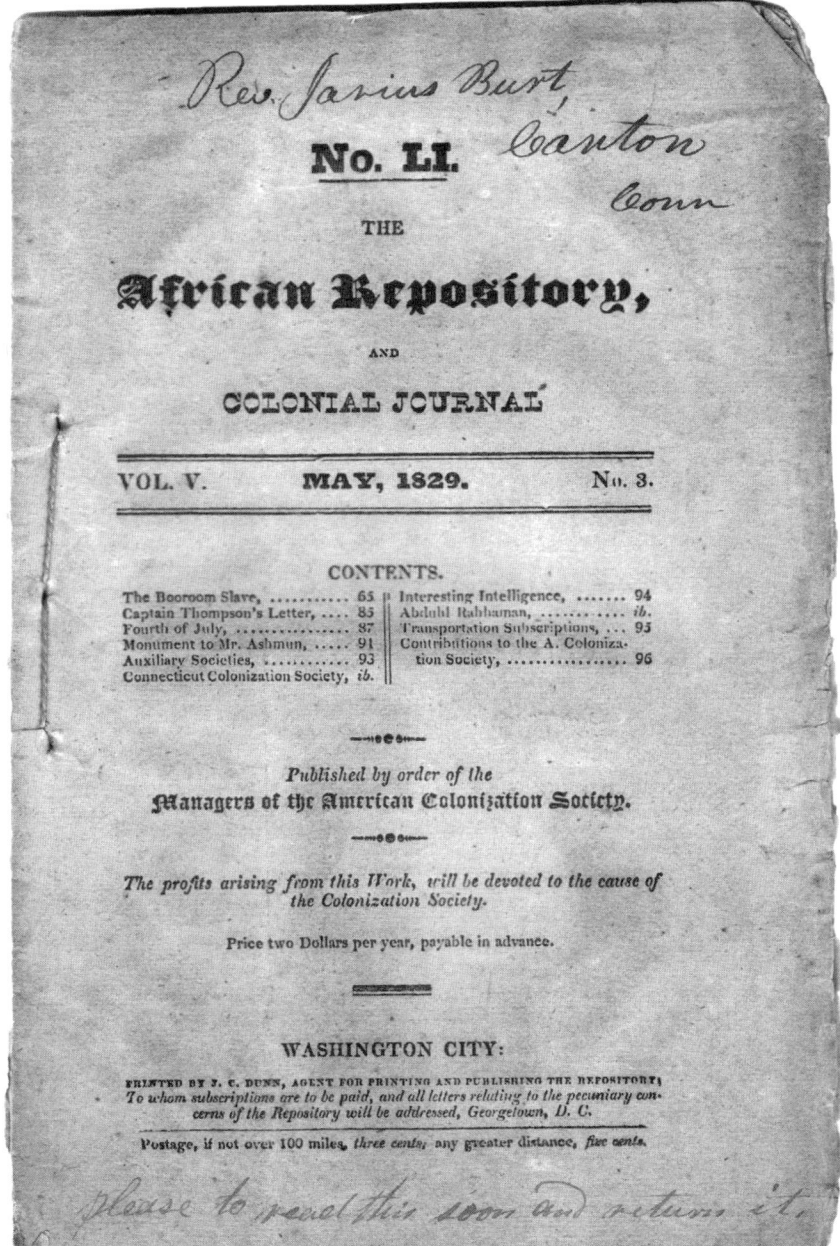

Issue of The African Repository and Colonial Journal (1829) from the McWorter family collection. Image courtesy of the McWorter family.

The McWorters were aggressive in buying land and establishing the economic basis for freedom. There were also other ex-slave families who were buying land as well. One of these was the Walkers, several of whom married McWorters. The Walker family came from Missouri, buying family members out of slavery and migrating to New Philadelphia.

Four generations of the McWorter family lived in New Philadelphia. This continuity is evidenced by the multiple collections of documents and photographs the McWorter family has handed down through the generations, collections that reflect the engagement of the McWorters with the world beyond New Philadelphia. Among the former are pamphlets about the institution of slavery, including an issue of *The African Repository and Colonial Journal*, published by the American Colonization Society. This organization promoted sending Black people back to Africa, and toward that end they established the country of Liberia for ex-slaves. That same year David Walker published his militant "Appeal to the Colored Citizens of the World."

Two more documents saved for posterity are sermons on the subject of slavery. One, from 1843, advocates using persuasion to end slavery: "If slavery in these states is abolished, the citizens of the States where it exists, must abolish it. They cannot be compelled. They must be persuaded." This was an advance in people's thinking beyond the idea of leaving the country. Another, from 1851, challenges the Fugitive Slave Act of 1850. This act of Congress called for the capturing of escaped slaves and their return to their former owners. This and the previous two documents indicate that the McWorters and by extension New Philadelphia were engaged in the core debates of the day over slavery and the evolving proposals for how it could be ended.

While they read and discussed these pamphlets, the McWorters were "practical abolitionists," in other words, they took action. Living McWorter descendants remember being shown a hiding place for freedom seekers in "the house that Frank built" across the road from New Philadelphia. An 1846 letter went from Frank to his son

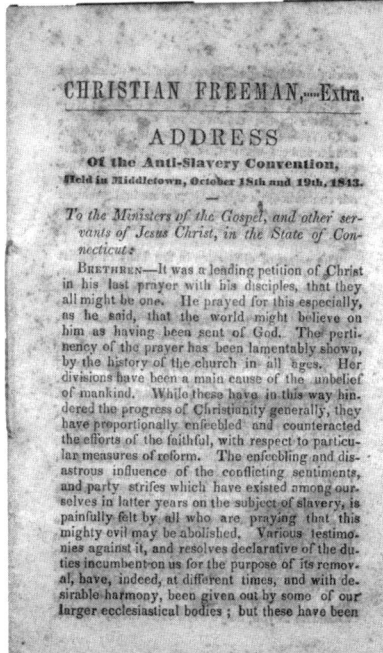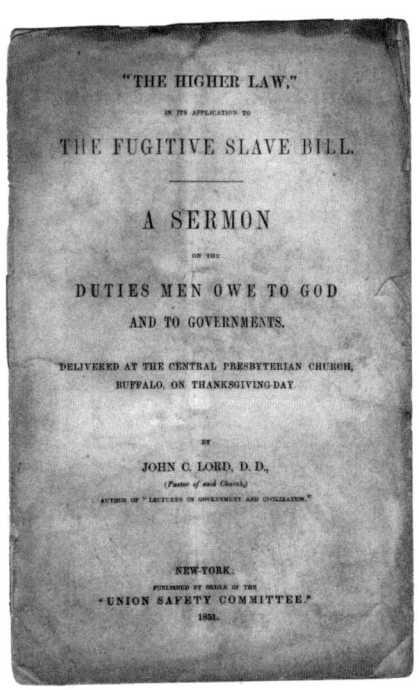

Sermons left to right, 1843 and 1851, McWorter family collection. Images courtesy of the McWorter family.

Frank, Jr still exists. Folded for delivery and addressed on the back of the sheet, it reads in part, "Squier and family are well and he said that you may look for him when you see him for he cannot tell when he can come to see you." Frank is most likely referring to a trip bringing fugitive slaves to Canada. An 1843 land mortgage document indicates Frank, Jr. owning a farm or a home on Talbot Middle Road, Rochester Township, Essex County. Since Frank the father could not read or write, he (like many others at the time) relied on someone else to write for him, and spelling was not yet standardized. As Charlotte King recounts:

> Solomon McWorter's son John, recounted that his father and uncles not only aided runaways, but sometimes accompanied them to Canada (Walker 1983:149, 168). It may have been on such a trip that young Frank met and returned to Illinois with Mary Ann, who is recorded on the 1850 census as Mary

> State of Illinois Pike Co. June 25th 1846
> Dear Son I take this oppertunity to informe you that we are all in common helth at presant and hope that these lines may find you injoying the same blesing of heaven Squier and famuly are well and he said that you may looke for him when you see him for he cannot tell when he can come to see you Solomon is at home and is working his land this Somewer Judy is at Quincy and the two youngest is at home and they all send you and your wife there respets and all desire to see you and your wife come and see us I have not time to right you but littel as Mr Jarry is in so grait a hurry that I can not right the cropes of wheat looke well and the people are harvisting So no more at presant but remain your affection at Father
> Francis McWhort
> N.B. wright as soon as you git this

Letter from Free Frank to Frank Jr in Canada. Helen McWorter Simpson papers, National Afro-American Museum and Cultural Center, Wilberforce University, Wilberforce, Ohio.

> A., a twenty-two year old white female born in England. Mary and two children, described on the census as a 3 year old mulatto female born in Canada and a 5 month old infant mulatto girl born in Illinois in the household of Squire and Louisa McWorter, young Frank's brother and sister-in-law (US Census 1850). (from King 2012, page 2)

As Helen McWorter Simpson wrote, Solomon was to become the

Solomon McWorter (1815–1879). Photo courtesy of the McWorter family.

anchor of the family in New Philadelphia and Pike County farming: "On the trip back to Pike County, father and son really got acquainted. 'Free Frank' explained to Solomon the great responsibility that would be his to take over from his father. He would have to work hard, deal fairly with his neighbor, and give back to the community part of what he received in money and service." (Unpublished manuscript, Helen McWorter Simpson papers, National Afro-American Museum and Cultural Center, Wilberforce University, Wilberforce, Ohio).

> "Solomon" was not as outgoing as his father. He was a grown man when his father purchased his freedom. The years

Solomon McWorter, the subject of this sketch, was born a slave, in the state of Kentucky, in the year 1815. He remained there, a slave, until the year 1835, when his father purchased him, and brought him to Illinois, where he has remained ever since. He was of good assistance to his father, in earning the money with which he purchased the family from slavery. He is now living on, and is the owner of, the old homestead, in Hadley township, where his father first settled. He is quite extensively engaged in farming and raising stock, and there are few men in Pike county who are succeeding better than he. In 1863, he married Miss Francis F. Coleman, of Springfield. She was born in the state of Missouri, in the year 1843, and emigrated to Illinois, with her parents, in 1856. They are now the parents of four children — one son and three daughters. Solomon's education is rather limited, but he is a man of good natural abilities, and very industrious, and is prospering well. He is now the owner of five hundred acres of first-class land, well stocked with cattle, hogs, horses, and mules. He is a man of good moral habits, and is highly respected by his neighbors.

Top, *Page from Helen McWorter Simpson's McWorter family history. Unpublished manuscript, Helen McWorter Simpson papers, National Afro-American Museum and Cultural Center, Wilberforce University, Wilberforce, Ohio.*
Bottom, *Description of Solomon McWorter from Ensign 1872 page 54. Public domain.*

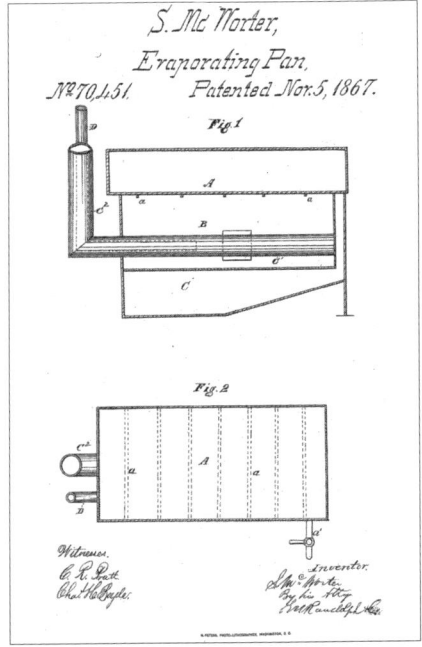 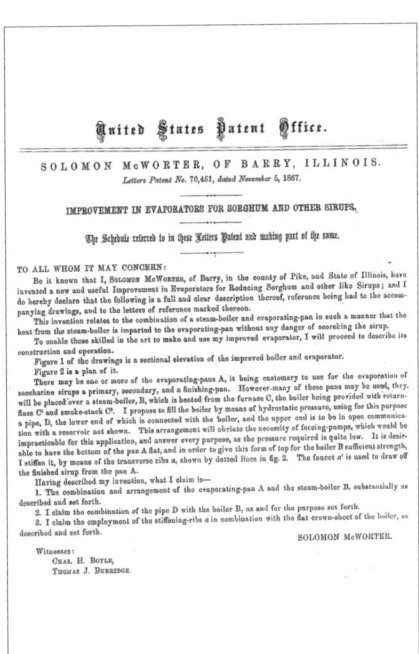

Right, Plans for sorghum evaporator patented by Solomon. ***Left***, Patent for improved sorghum evaporator awarded to Solomon McWorter in 1867. United States Patent Office documents in public domain.

The McWorter family achieved a great deal in the 1830s, 1840s, and 1850s, while simultaneously saving up to purchase family members and aiding others along their way. One remaining 1840s land deed has Solomon and his much younger brother Squire buying land from the neighboring Shipman family. Newspaper accounts mention Solomon driving his cattle to the railroad stop in Barry as well as shipping apples up the Mississippi to Minnesota.

As with farming and the Underground Railroad, the family's industriousness connected with their impulse towards freedom. The patent awarded to Solomon in 1867 was for a pan that would more readily evaporate sorghum syrup. He had likely been growing and processing sorghum for some years by the time the patent was approved. Suitable to a more temperate climate, sorghum arrived in the United States in the 1850s from China and France, and was fa-

Letter from Solomon McWorter to Frances Jane Coleman, September 1863. Image from Simpson 1981, page 23.

vored by abolitionists locally and elsewhere who boycotted "blood-stained sugar" and other goods made by slave labor. Solomon was the first African American to get a patent in Illinois and the eighth nationwide. His address is given as Barry, Illinois, because the post office for New Philadelphia closed in 1853.

Solomon married Frances Jane Coleman on September 29, 1863. Earlier that month he had written to her:

> I intend to come over about 26th of this month and I hope you will be ready to get married so I will not have to leave you again for you are the one I truly love. I cannot express my feelings toward you in writing so I will not try. I would like it if we could get married on Tuesday and get home on Thurs-

58 NEW PHILADELPHIA

Frances Jane McWorter. Photo courtesy of the McWorter family.

> day if it would be according to your feelings. Tuesday is the 29th of this month I believe. Any arrangement that you want made write to me, I want you to feel that our interests are one. It will be a pleasure to me to make you happy.

At the time of their marriage he was 48 and she was 20. Together they had eight children, the first born in a log cabin and the rest born in a frame house that Solomon built. Jane became one of the matriarchs of the McWorter family, even after she remarried a decade after Solomon's death, until her own death in 1925.

Solomon and Jane's oldest son was John. He was a scientist and engineer by nature, but losing his father at age 15, he stayed on the family's New Philadelphia farm to help his mother until his brothers Frank and Arthur could assume responsibilities. Mostly self-educat-

Left, John McWorter. Photo by Wickiser, North Springfield, Missouri, courtesy of the McWorter family.

Right, Sarah McWorter, Frank and Lucy's third child, gained her freedom at age 32. Photo used with permission of the family; from the New Philadelphia Collection found in Newton, Kansas by descendant Conle White.

ed, he helped invent the helicopter. He won three patents (United States patents nos. 1,114,167; 1,115,710; and 1,438,929) on a flying machine that the War Department came to see in flight in 1919.

Sarah McWorter, Frank and Lucy's third child, was 32 years old when Frank returned to Kentucky to purchase her freedom. An Illinois court record that was entered into the records in Pulaski County, Kentucky, reveals something about this achievement. This record served as proof that she was entitled to her freedom:

> I Henry J. Mudd clerk of Pike Co Illinois commissioner's court ... certify that ...on Monday the 4th of September 1843 Frank McWorter produced to said court ... a deed of emancipation ... setting free Sally McWorter a woman of color of yellow complexion aged about 35 years of age. Said Sally be-

ing a slave and formerly owned by Obediah Denham of Pulaski Co Kentucky.... appears from said deed so emancipation has been purchased by the said Frank McWorter of the said Denham....subscribed and sealed by Frank McWorter and bears date the said 5 September 1843 and was acknowledged by said McWorter before the ... open court to be his act and deed. HJ Mudd clerk. Certified by John Neely Sr judge of court Pike Co Illinois. (From the recorded deeds of Pulaski County, Kentucky, volume 12 page 378. Text courtesy of http://kykinfolk.org/pulaski/poc/trans.html)

Frank's trip to liberate Sarah was his second such journey from Illinois to Kentucky. He could not read, but he carried documents with him that validated his own freedom. In family oral history, he also carried a gun in case the power of his paper needed assistance. The price of Sarah's freedom in 1843 was $950, which would be $30,000 in 2015 dollars.

While in slavery Sarah had five children. As testimony to the unbroken connection between the free and not-yet-free McWorter siblings, Sarah named one of her children born into slavery after her then-12-year-old sister Lucy Ann, born free and then living in Illinois. In 1843 when Sarah gained her freedom, she had to leave the five children she had borne by then in Kentucky. But over time the family managed to free each child.

Thirteen years after she became free and just one month after a probate court released funds that Frank McWorter's will specifically allocated for this purpose, Sarah traveled back to Kentucky. In just four days, she was able to buy three of her children from three different men. Lucy Ann, Calvin, and Hiley were 26, 23, and 20 years old. The freedom papers record their mother's negotiations. The back of Calvin's purchase document includes the text, "I hereby manumit and set free the person within named. Sarah McWorter X her mark Attest H. Barbin." This indicates that Sarah could not read. And still she succeeded! One can only imagine the challenges she met along the way.

Sarah lived from 1811 to 1891, raising six children that we know of, and was buried in New Philadelphia. Three of them survived her; her gravestone mentions only two because before it could be made,

Top, Freedom documents of Lucy Ann, Calvin, and Hiley McWorter. Images courtesy of the McWorter family via Zelia Alberta McWorter Ewing.

Left, Sarah McWorter in Kansas, where she lived with her daughter Hiley and son-in-law Alexander Clark, and Sarah McWorter's gravestone. Photos courtesy of the McWorter family.

one of those three passed away. Sarah experienced the explosive growth of slavery and also its end and aftermath. She saw New Philadelphia grow into a town, and persist after the town was dissolved into an informal settlement.

In the end, Juda, who was named for her African grandmother, had the longest life as a freed person and outlived all her siblings, passing away in 1906 at age 105. She saw her father's mission achieved: several grandchildren freed, two more fighting in the Civil War, slavery abolished and the McWorter family living free and farming their own land. One of her children, Charlotte, was purchased by the family using funds allocated for that purpose by her brother Commodore in a codicil, or supplement, to his will. A remarkable letter provided on pages 159-160 of Juliet Walker's book provides some background to that purchase. She tells the story in even greater detail, but here is the letter William Denham wrote to Solomon McWorter:

> 1854 December the 30 Somerset Ky
>
> dear Sir I take my pen in hand this morning with Sorrow in my hart to let you no that I Cannot prevent my father from Selling Sharlet I have kept him from Selling hur for too years I Can doo nothing more with him if you want hur you had Better Come quick you ned not tak of the River being frose up if you want Sharlet Come Right [a]long
>
> I Right this unbe[known] to my father; you Can by hur for $850, or 900 hur and hur Child I think Carlet has got as purty A Child and as Smart as I Ever have Seen white or Black and it is all most white I feel anctious you would Come and Buy hur the Children is all weell the mail is a bout to start and I must Come to a close Beshore to Come on Right Soon
>
> Your friend
>
> William Denham

Hiley K. McWorter Clark, Sarah McWorter's daughter, lived in New Philadelphia after getting free. She married Alexander Clark, giving birth to nine children and also raising his two surviving chil-

Top left, Hiley K. McWorter Clark. Photo used with permission of the family; from the New Philadelphia Collection found in Newton, Kansas by descendant Conle White, great-grandson of Hiley McWorter Clark.
Top right, Charlotte's only daughter, mentioned in the letter on page 63, was Judy Cowan. Photo courtesy of Karen Wall.
Right, Calvin McWorter. Photo courtesy of the McWorter family.

dren from a previous marriage. Then in 1873 several McWorters and Clarks moved to Valley Center, Kansas. All Hiley's children are buried there, except Lucy Ann Brooks in Jacksonville, Illinois.

Calvin McWorter (1839–1893) Sarah McWorter's son, moved to Kansas along with his sister and other relatives. The freedom impulse that brought people to New Philadelphia also propelled them farther west. Just as Frank sold his Kentucky farm for Illinois land, others may have done the same thing to get from Illinois to Kansas. Calvin eventually owned a 1200-acre farm in Kansas. He was the McWorter who in the 1880s told a historian that his great-grandmother gave birth to his grandfather Frank, wrapped him in her apron, and carried him into the house to show the master. And we know that master was also Frank's father. This glimpse helps us imagine the personal experience of the inhumanity of slavery in the United States. It shows as well the persistence of memory and respect for the family's achievements.

Burnham of Barry, Illinois was perhaps the closest photographer to New Philadelphia, and took the photograph on the next page of an unidentified McWorter family member. This and many of the others in this book appear in more than one family collection, because it was customary to order multiple prints from the photographer and then send them to relatives and close friends as an expression of affection. Although it is rare to see someone's name written on the back of the photo, these overlapping family collections often helped identify someone. Her expression conveys the strength and health that most of the McWorters must have had. The appearance of this photo in multiple collections also suggests that she and other McWorters consistently reached out to relatives and friends in order to be safe and succeed in their farming and their freedom mission.

Unidentified McWorter family member. Photo courtesy of the McWorter family.

Chapter Three

Town

New Philadelphia was the first town in the United States established by a successful family of African American freedmen and -women. Family patriarch Frank McWorter saw that the town was platted and legally registered even before he obtained the legislation that secured his own right to do business in the state, and three decades before the end of slavery. But at least two other towns deserve mention alongside New Philadelphia. First, Brooklyn, Illinois, across the Mississippi River from St. Louis. Black people first settled here in the 1820s and it too became a center for practical abolitionism and the Underground Railroad. A European-American platted Brooklyn in 1837. Its freedom tradition was so strong that in 1891 residents renamed the town Lovejoy, honoring the minister, journalist, newspaper editor and abolitionist who was murdered in 1837 by a proslavery mob in nearby Alton, Illinois. It is easy to imagine personal connections between 1800s Brooklyn and New Philadelphia.

The second town to mention is Nicodemus, Kansas. This town was established after the Civil War in 1877 by a group of African Americans and one European American. The oldest Black settlement west of the Mississippi River, it attracted freed slaves after the War. Many sought land and life in the free state of Kansas. New Philadelphians who migrated westward from Illinois settled in Kansas, although not in Nicodemus.

From the start, like these other African American communities, New Philadelphia was a freedom village. New Philadelphians actively opposed slavery in at least seven ways. First, many residents had run for freedom. Second, they purchased each other's freedom. Third, they worked hard and long and invested carefully. In the booming land market of the 1800s the town lots and nearby farms were a way to accumulate money to buy family members and others out of slavery. Fourth, the town was a station on the Underground Railroad, hiding people and helping them escape north from slavery, just 20 miles from the Mississippi River and the slave state of Missouri. The river was an artery moving goods and people, including those escaping. An analysis of United States and Illinois Census data shows the town as home to between 14 to 48 African Americans over the years, comprising over time between 17% and 38% of the population. Fifth, the town was named New Philadelphia: a new City of Brotherly Love. This name was a clear anti-slavery and pro-equality message. Sixth, various sons of New Philadelphia, of all colors, fought for the North in the Civil War. Finally, they lived free: New Philadelphia attracted both African and European descendants, armed and living in proximity, many on their own land. Moreover, many of those families chose to settle there for generations, at a time when economic, political, and moral struggles over slavery were tearing at the very soul and fabric of the society.

What conditions of life did they find when they arrived, and how did they survive? Terry and Claire Martin (2010, page 85) explain:

> An 1880 Pike County history (Chapman 1880:282–287,345) provides impressions of the wildlife "Free" Frank McWorter and the early residents of New Philadelphia found when they arrived in the 1830s. Gray fox, cougar, black bear, and white-tailed deer became rare soon after the area was settled, whereas opossum, raccoon, muskrat, eastern cottontail, and tree squirrels remained common. Wolves threatened livestock, resulting in bounties and organized wolf hunts. Birds of special note were wild turkey, prairie chicken, ruffed grouse, bobwhite, Carolina parakeet, passenger pigeon, and many species of ducks and geese. The Mississippi and Illinois rivers were "quite prolific" with fish, and species of economic

European-Americans	97
From free states	68
From slave states	21
From Great Britain or Canada (free)	7
Unknown origin	1
African-Americans	4
All	101

Year	New Philadelphia		Illinois
	All	African-American	African-American
1850	58	22 (38%)	5,000 (0.6%)
1855	81	81 (22%)	
1860	114	21 (18%)	7,628 (0.4)
1865	160	48 (30%)	
1870	123	31 (25%)	28,762 (1.1)
1880	84	14 (17%)	46,368 (1.5%)

Top, Hadley Township population in 1850. Data from 1850 U.S. Census. *Bottom*, New Philadelphia population, 1850–1880. Data from King 2006 and 1850 U.S. Census.

importance included suckers, such as buffalo and redhorse, channel catfish and bullheads, and paddlefish. Despite the abundance of wild game, the dietary staple in Pike County soon became "pork and poultry" (Chapman 1880:345).

Even as the laws of Illinois were proslavery, Hadley Township (where New Philadelphia was located) reflected Northern as well as Southern origins. A tally of the township's resident landowners as of

1850 shows that by far the largest number were born in free states. Among them were known abolitionists. The state's population was sharply divided regarding slavery and freedom.

The U.S. and Illinois Census data shows population shifts in New Philadelphia over the town's history. This data suggests that the town, founded by a black man, always attracted a large percent of African Americans, but an even larger percent of European-Americans. Chicago itself only reached this high a percentage of African Americans after the Great Migrations of the 20th century. What makes New Philadelphia's population profile even more remarkable is that Illinois was a Northern state with strong proslavery sentiment and Black Code laws.

New Philadelphia's life as an official town spanned from 1836 to 1885. As King analyses it, the local population peaked at 160 people. There is no record of any racist violence in New Philadelphia, although it undoubtedly contained a diverse mix of opinion and behavior. The town was a lively place, with a post office, a school, a general store, a blacksmith, two shoemakers or cobblers. It hosted Sunday religious services. It was a hub for surrounding farming families. One of Free Frank's projects was to establish a seminary to train ministers. This would have meant schooling beyond the basic reading, writing, and arithmetic, even beyond high school. The plan did not work out, but a subsequent lawsuit left us with evidence identifying at least some of the parties involved.

> As a boy I attended the school known as the New Philadelphia School. [...] we were fortunate in having several teachers in our school who had a high school or college training, so that there were introduced into this country school several high school studies. Physics, or Natural Phillosophy, was it was called then, was one of them. (from a biographical statement by John E. McWorter, 1864-1927, in the Helen McWorter Simpson Collection in the archives of the National Afro-American Museum and Cultural Center, Wilberforce, Ohio)

This focus on education surely encouraged many young New Philadelphians to continue their education at Barry High School; at

New Philadelphia, mid-1800s. Photo courtesy of the McWorter family.

the abolitionist Mission Institute in Quincy; in Springfield, IL; and beyond.

Urbanization was one force keeping New Philadelphia small. Chris Fennell concludes that the town may also have missed a possibility for growth when the Hannibal and Naples Railroad was routed not through the town but around it, farther north even than many maps from the period indicate. The chosen route cost more to build, being longer and with less favorable terrain. The decision makers were slave owning elites in Hannibal, Missouri. Alternative explanations of the train routing and impact are voiced by some and historians continue to research the question, but Fennell's published research is detailed in chapter 4.

Even as a small Midwestern village, New Philadelphia was connected from the start to the national economy. Some settlers came from the nation's big East Coast cities, bringing items manufactured there and in Europe. Travelers of all sorts passed through New Philadelphia, and New Philadelphians themselves traveled. National and global connections also came from being just 20 miles from the Mis-

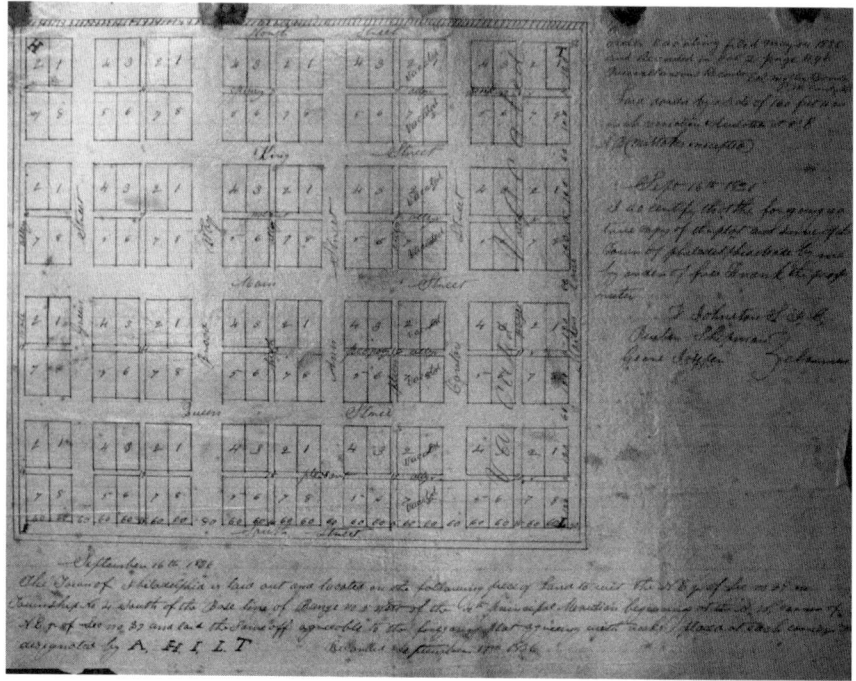

Plat of New Philadelphia. Image courtesy of the McWorter family.

sissippi River. The river was an artery for global commerce, a thruway based on the slave trade and before that the trade with and exploitation of Native Americans on what was then the western frontier.

The previous page shows one of the few actual photos we have of early New Philadelphia. Four things identify this scene as New Philadelphia. First, the landscape. Fruit trees were cultivated in the area by the mid-1800s. Second, the log houses are typical of the time and place. Third, the African American family. Finally the fact that the photograph is part of two different family collections: that of Gerald McWorter and that of Karen Wall. Gerald is descended from McWorters who stayed in New Philadelphia until the 1950s. Karen is a genealogist and grandmother of a McWorter descendant in Kansas. Karen's copy of the photo was handed down from Calvin McWorter's family to descendants Charles and Dee Porter and then to her. Calvin had left New Philadelphia by the 1880s. At the time of this photo, Kansas was almost treeless and people lived in houses made of sod or dug half into the ground unless they could import lumber, in which case it was not logs but planks, so the Kansas descendants knew that it could not be Kansas.

On the facing page is the official record of the survey laying out the town of New Philadelphia. Its accuracy was proven more than a century later by the work of Likes Land Surveyors. Frank McWorter hired a surveyor to divide some of his land into town lots that he could sell, across the road from his own house. Reuben Shipman, signing here in an official capacity, was the head of another abolitionist landowning family who lived and farmed land adjacent to the McWorters for many decades. (Reuben's own family patriarch Edward arrived from England to Connecticut in 1639.) Not all 140 lots were occupied, but many were sold, some as many as 12 times over the lifetime of the town. Both African Americans and European Americans bought and sold lots. As settlers arrived and local and county improvements were made, the value of the land generally increased over this time.

The two maps on the next pages show the town and who owned land across Hadley Township. The railroad is shown without great accuracy; it was not built until 1869 and even the later map may have only estimated its location. Each numbered section is one mile wide. In addition to the McWorters, other ex-slave families were buying land: one, the Walkers, became linked with the McWorters through several marriages. Hadsells, Burdicks, Iricks, Shipmans, Clarks, Walkers, and Vonds can all be found here. These two maps can be compared to the 1912 map in chapter 4.

European and African Americans in New Philadelphia associated in realms beyond the commercial. For example, there is archaeological evidence of mancala, which was and is a game played all over Africa and the Arab world that involves moving pieces around a set of holes in a board or even in the ground. Pieces found at New Philadelphia—for more see Chapter 6—establish that both African American and European American households played this game.

When the time came, they joined together in the war to end

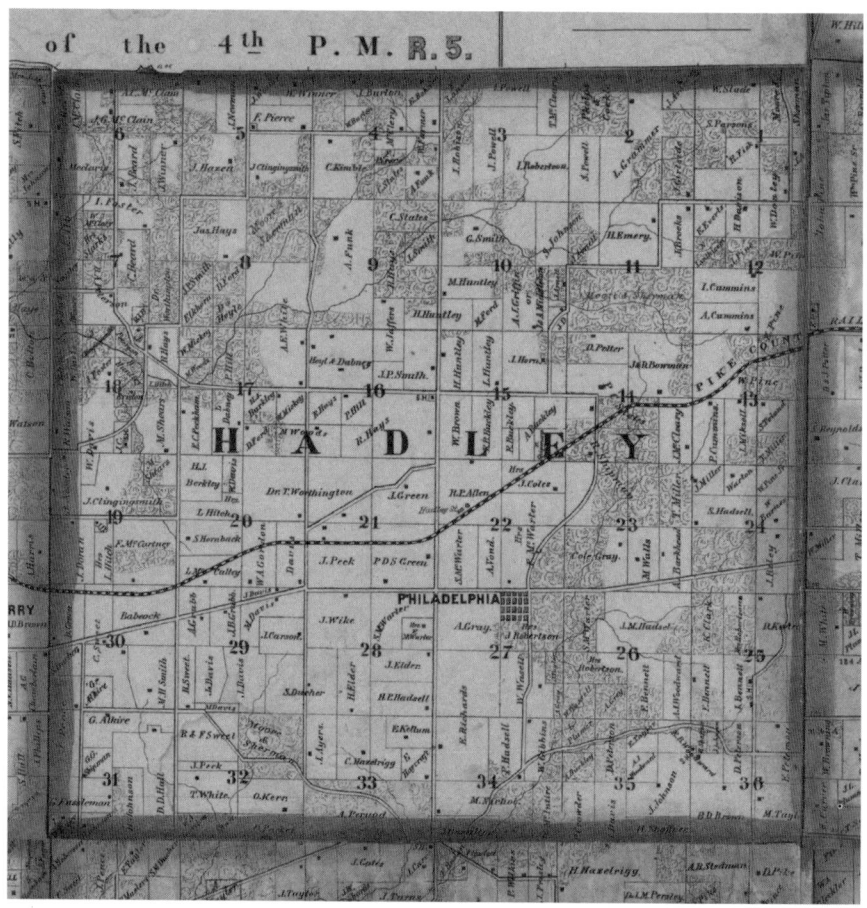

New Philadelphia in 1860. Detail from Map of Pike County, Illinois *published in 1860 by Holmes & Arnold, Buffalo, New York. Image from Library of Congress, Geography and Map Division. Public domain.*

slavery, although the army in which they enlisted kept them apart. Young men who grew up together in New Philadelphia and the surrounding area had to join separate Union Army units based on their color. The United States War Department established the Bureau of Colored Troops in May 1863, two years after the Civil War began. Three Union Civil War veterans, Squire McWorter, Jr., Thomas Clark, and Martin Kimbro, are buried in the McWorter cemetery. Squire (grandson of Free Frank) and a fourth known veteran Sime-

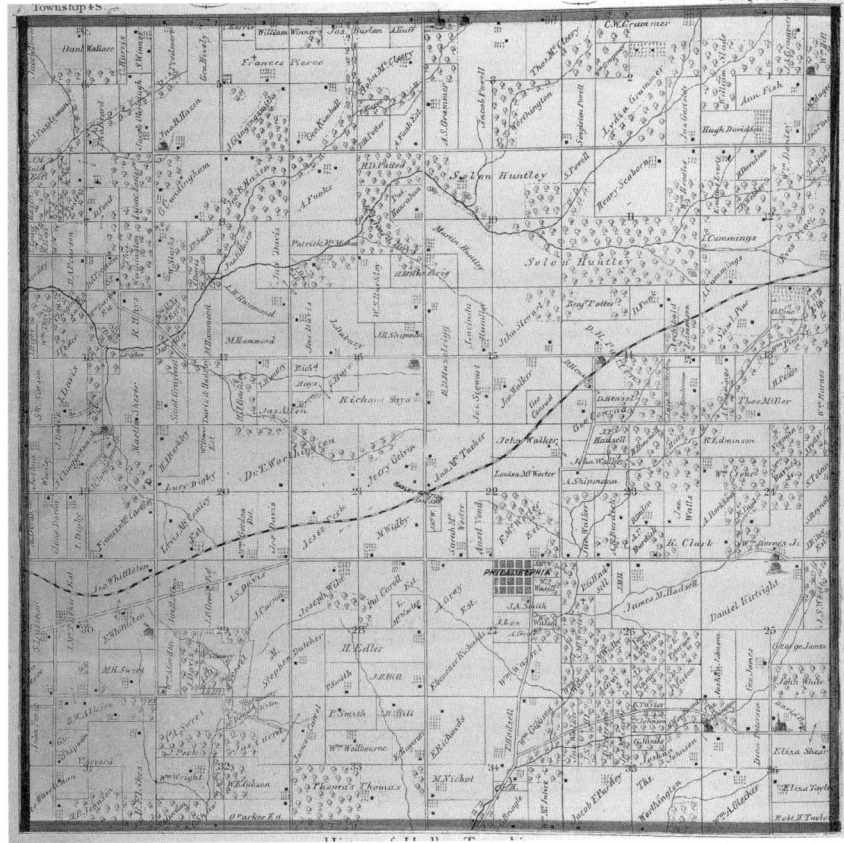

New Philadelphia in 1872. D. W. Ensign, Atlas Map of Pike County, Illinois, *Davenport, Iowa: Andreas, Lyter & Co., 1872, p. 100. Public domain.*

on Clark served in the United States Colored Troops 38th Infantry Regiment in 1865; Simeon migrated to Kansas. The graves of Thomas Clark and Kimbro have star markers, the design of which refers to the fighting with the images of a bugle, two cannons with six balls, crossed rifles, crossed swords, and the Christian symbol of an anchor. These grave markers were placed by the Grand Army of the Republic, which was the fraternal organization of Civil War veterans. Unlike the segregated United States armed forces of the war, the GAR had integrated chapters, or posts, and fought for voting rights for Black

Mancala game board, Sierra Leone. Photo by Brooklyn Museum, Creative Commons BY license.

veterans. Thomas Clark was active in the Quincy, Illinois, GAR.

Yet even while the town of New Philadelphia was small and integrated, it had two cemeteries. Some two dozen people are known to be buried in one and close to 100 in the other. Verifying whether these were totally segregated is a task for future historians, but today they are known as the McWorter cemetery and the Johnson cemetery. Items found resting on the McWorter graves include shells and light colored glass, signifying the spirit world in West African traditions and often found on older African American graves. The location of the cemetery across a creek from the town and the orientation of the graves towards the creek connect to the tradition of water as a spirit pathway back to Africa.

European-Americans Abel R. Burdick and Philander Hadsell each farmed just west of New Philadelphia, as the 1872 map in chapter 2 shows. They were both buried in the Johnson cemetery, among family members.

The documentary record evidences the transactions that served to knit New Philadelphia into the economy and political structure of the county, the state, and the nation. Until the end of the Civil War, freedom papers were an important document for African American residents of the town. Slavery was legal in Illinois until 1848 and the Black Codes existed until 1865. In 1844 John T. Jones, the prominent

Top left, Button from coat or jacket of Union soldier found at New Philadelphia, likely one of the four veterans from the town. Photo courtesy of the Illinois State Museum
Top right, Star marking the grave of either Thomas Clark or Martin Kimbro, New Philadelphia. Photo by Gary Andresko, courtesy of Paul Shackel.
Middle left, McWorter Cemetery. Photo by Claire Martin, used with permission.
Middle right, Gravestone of Abel R. Burdick, Johnson cemetery. Photo of gravestone in Johnson cemetery courtesy of Ron & Chris at findagrave.com.
Left, Gravestone of Phineas Hadsell, Johnson cemetery. Photo of gravestone in Johnson cemetery courtesy of Ron & Chris at findagrave.com.

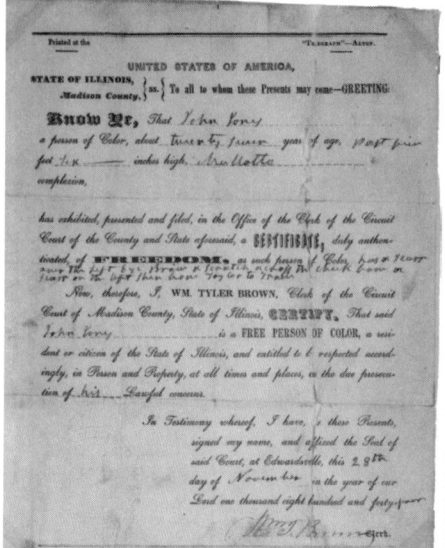 

Left, Circuit Court certificate of the freedom of John T. Jones. Photo used with permission of Chicago History Museum.
Right, John T. Jones of Chicago. Photo from Hayes 1897, page 191. Public domain.

Illinois abolitionist and campaigner against the Black Codes, went to the Madison County Circuit Court and obtained the certificate of freedom shown here. Documents like this one were sought after and kept safe by African Americans living in New Philadelphia. They were at least partial protection against kidnapping and legal harassment.

Although many people in the 18th and 19th century United States could not read or write, the written record was important. One purpose was keeping friends, neighbors, and local businesses clear on financial details. The surviving financial record suggests many kinds of economic interactions among residents of New Philadelphia. Typical for the time, the receipt here states that Spaulding Burdick has received "payment in full from Frank McWorter of all demands [debts] to this date." On three separate occasions, Spaulding, who was a shoemaker as well as a farmer, bought New Philadelphia town lots from Frank McWorter. Remaining until the 1970s,

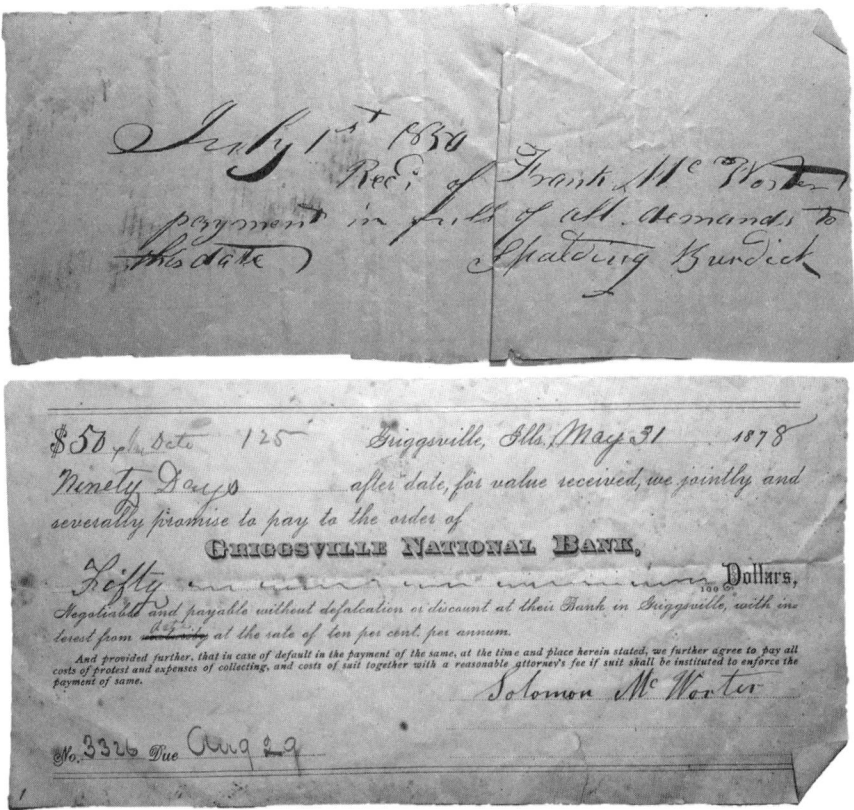

Top, Record of transaction between Frank McWorter and Spaulding Burdick dated July 1, 1850. Photo courtesy of the McWorter family.
Bottom, Promissory note of Solomon McWorter held by the Griggsville National Bank. Photo courtesy of the McWorter family.

the Burdick family appears to be the last family from the days of New Philadelphia the town to live and farm there. More of their story is told in Chapter 4.

Individuals transacted business with local institutions as well as with each other. A May 31, 1878 loan by the Griggsville National Bank to Solomon McWorter of New Philadelphia included 10% interest over a period of three months. With the loan due in August, it may well have been to help pay for equipment for the growing season. The bank was 14 miles to the east.

The most important connections in the town, however, were

within and between families. As mentioned above, the Shipmans were a leading New Philadelphia family who worked together with the McWorters. Reuben and Clarissa Shipman from Connecticut owned a farm just outside New Philadelphia by the early 1830s, where they raised their family. At least one son, Alfred, continued the farm. Another, William, graduated from Quincy's abolitionist Mission Institute. Reuben witnessed and certified documents for the McWorters, and the Shipmans sold land in Derry township south of New Philadelphia to Squire and Solomon McWorter. When Free Frank McWorter passed away in 1854 at age 77, George Conrad, son-in-law to Reuben and Clarissa Shipman, along with Mary and Sarah Thomas, who were McWorters, witnessed Frank McWorter's last will and testament.

Clarissa Shipman wrote a steady stream of letters to her family back east and later to son William and daughter-in-law Jane. William and Jane met at the Mission Institute in Quincy, Illinois, married and became missionaries in Hawaii. Her letters were full of New Philadelphia news, and one passage reveals how close the McWorters and the Shipmans were, telling of one way they joined in anti-slavery activism:

> Your cousin Solomon [McWorter] is very busy making molasses from Chinese sugar cane [i.e. sorghum] which he raised on thirteen acres of his land. He makes about a barrel a day which fetches sixteen dollars. It is excellent if made good. So you see we are getting quite independent of the South as to our sweetening." (Shipman Letter Collection, quoted in Cahill 1996, page 57)

Barbara Anderson of Hilo, Hawaii, is Clarissa's great-great-great-granddaughter. Barbara made the Shipman Letter Collection available. Descendant Mel Conrad of Kensington, Minnesota sent copies and transcriptions of letters from Clarissa in his possession. He also shared a 1912 obituary of Clarissa's son-in-law that identified him as a man who "helped escaping slaves to freedom." We found one more letter in the collection of the Winterthur Museum, Garden and Library in Delaware and obtained an image of it. Altogether these

Left to right, Reuben, Clarissa, William and Jane Shipman. Photos used with permission of W. H. Shipman.

letters are well worth including here.

Clarissa's letters tell of the origins of New Philadelphia, including this to her relative Betsey North in 1836:

> I just want to let you know how people get along here. We have a neighbor free Frank they call him. He came to this country about five years ago. He exchanged a small place he had in Kentucky for 160 acres of land and after he got into the country he had to stop and work to live through the winter for he had not a dollar left. He went on to Kentucky last summer and paid $550 for one of his sons that was a slave in that country. He has now got 480 acres considerable under improvement quite a large stock of cattle with about a dozen horses which are valuable in this country. In short he is worth between $4000 and five thousand dollars and Frank paid about $3000 for his own liberty and his wife and three sons. He has now two daughters in bondage. (Letter courtesy of Mel Conrad)

Around the same time she writes to "Sister" Sophie:

> There is a prospect of having a town near us. Frank our colored neighbor is about having one laid out. His object is to raise money to redeem his two daughters who are yet in slavery. I hope he may succeed. (Letter courtesy of Mel Conrad)

Her 1860s letters, all from the Shipman Letter Collection, describe local events as the nation approaches the Civil War. In a letter to her children dated May 21, 1860 she describes the hard conditions of life in the New Philadelphia area. This is six years after the death of Frank McWorter:

> the past two or three seasons have been very discouraging and the prospect for the future is anything but encouraging from the fact that the prospect for market is so poor. Although the season has been poor for farming it has on the whole been very pleasant although we have food, our wheat stack burned. I don't think we shall suffer for want of bread and we have enough of everything else for comfort but we have neighbors who have been without bread of any kind even corn bread in their families for weeks and others if we may believe report who had no kind of food but corn bread and some who would have been glad of even that and these are sober respectable industrious hardworking people. Rags and patches and shoes and clothes on their feet are very fashionable. I never heard of so much complaint of a country and I don't know whether there was ever so much dissatisfaction and disappointment among the settlers of any country. Almost everyone seems to be in the same condemnation no matter how hard a man works, how close he scrubs, how well he calculates, he gets nothing or next to it. Those who have been here longest are worst off and those who brought money are no better off than those that came without. A sorry picture is it not.

Clarissa is also focused on telling how Civil War issues and conflicts are unfolding in Illinois, the state of Abraham Lincoln. The same letter speaks to a division of abolitionists and proslavery forces in the New Philadelphia area. She compares how freedom seekers were guided to freedom in the area by abolitionists, and then captured back into slavery by those she calls secessionists:

> We have had stirring times here lately. Half a dozen of our neighbors caught four fugitives. Slaves from Missouri and carried them back to their masters for which it is said they got twelve hundred dollars. Some say less. It is the first time they have had the luck to catch one although they have tried

before. There seems to be pretty good reason to believe that they enticed them off and brought them as far as the burying ground in Barry where they were set down and told they could go where they pleased as they were among friends. They had got out on the Griggsville road when they went out and took them. It was upon the Sabbath. There did not seem to be anybody that knew it until it was all over. Two of the esquire Grubbs sons and Goodrich Stoats were the principal ones. Grubb is judge of our Court of Probate. I think we have fallen on evil times.

On November 1, 1861, after the start of the war, she describes how armed conflict challenges were part of the local experience in Illinois:

We have had quite peaceable times hereabouts since the commencement of the war but I think should the Secessionists carry Mo. We should see trouble. I think there is not much danger at present. I do not know that we have many Secessionists in this neighborhood. C. Stoats is a rabid one and I expect it would go hard with us could he have his way. He has expressed his views pretty freely, said he wanted to get a shot at a few Abolitionist neighbors. Dr. Baker gave him to understand that he was watched and should there be any mischief done he would fare hard, which frightened considerably. It is said he keeps three loaded guns standing by his bed for use should he be disturbed. He has been quiet of late. They have had two fights at Pittsfield and Barry but it was over before we heard of it. Word came Sunday evening while people were at meeting that the rebels were threatening Louisiana [Missouri] & they wanted all the men they could get, the men turned out pretty well....Fitch left the meeting went home got his gun & was back as soon as the rest were ready. The enemy decamped as soon as they found they were to be met by a number of determined Union men. They have been very badly frightened at Quincy once or twice but after calling out the home guards & sending to Springfield for

> troops they concluded there was not as much danger as they apprehended, but if the Secessionists of Missouri should carry their point I think they would feel as if they had some old scores to settle with us on this side of the river....You will perhaps be surprised to hear that Mr. Nesmith is a secessionist & that his son Jimmie is an officer in the rebel army. Mr. N. is living in Canton, Mo. The last I heard of him he was a cripple. He had been confined to his bed for more than a year. He lost his wife a number of years ago & afterward married a daughter of Mr. Bush who died some two years ago. He is now a widower. None of your friends have gone to the war but a few from hereabouts. Mr. Grey has two stepsons in the army, his sons & three or four of his daughters are in Kansas. Mr. Flurt has raised a company about Barry. He is stationed I believe at Pilot Knob.

Freedom seekers helped harvest crops in the area. The army created a new term for them, contrabands, as they had stolen themselves from planters in rebel territory. She recounts in November 25, 1862:

> I do not know what we are coming to. The prospect...the Democrats have got the majority in a number of the states ours among the rest in the last election and I suppose they will try to break up the government but there is consolation in knowing that we are in the hands of God and that nothing can take place without his permission should he in infinite wisdom see fit to give us up in our extremity. He would be just. We deserve it all, for we are verily guilty concerning our brother but may God in mercy send deliverance and save our beloved country. Our farmers are sadly in want of help as so many of our laborers have gone to war. The contrabands I suppose would come in in considerable numbers were they allowed. A man two or three miles south of here employed a few. It is said a number of men proslaveryites were going to mob him. He got his arms ready and a few of his neighbors together and showed such a determined front that they left thinking I suppose that discretion was the better part of val-

or. I have not heard of their molesting him since.

While there were many proslavery forces in the area, and of course over the Mississippi River in Missouri, the area itself was pro-Union with active abolitionist in the area. This incident she recounts demonstrates this:

> G. Stoats is a very strong secessionist. He made so many threats last spring of shooting abolitionists as he called all Union men that. The states Marshall undertook to arrest him but being from home he got wind of it and absented himself and was gone some six or seven weeks but he is now home again. Some of his neighbors I know breathed easier when he was gone. But I think he will not molest anybody at present.

On a more personal level, she repeatedly shared news of the McWorters with her offspring in Hawaii. On April 26, 1862 Clarissa writes, "They are well at Aunt Lucy, what there is left of them. There is none of them there but Solomon and Sally with two of her family. Aunt Lucy has been very sick. They thought she could not get up again but she looks very bright and smart now." On December 3, 1862 she comments:

> Aunt Lucy [then 91] is still living and pretty smart. She don't seem to grow old much although I suppose she is considerably over ninety. When I was very sick last summer, she came up afoot to see me. She spent the day here and rode home at night with Doctor Baker.

And on January 20, 1865 she reports:

> Jane will be so near she can come to see me if I cannot go to see her. Aunt Lucy has been sick but is getting better. She bears her age remarkably well. I suppose she must be nearly a hundred years old if not over. Solomon has an heir, a smart little fellow. He lives in the house with his mother. Sally has bought a place in Philadelphia and has moved there. Judy has lost her husband. She lives in Jacksonville but is here very often. She looks almost as old as her mother.

The smart little fellow was John McWorter.

The Clarks were another family with close ties to the McWort-

County record concerning the last will and testament of Free Frank McWorter. Photo courtesy of Kathy Robinson, from the Pike County Courthouse records. Public domain.

ers. The family matriarch was Kesiah Clark, who bought at least one lot from Frank and Lucy McWorter, paying $5 in 1854. Kesiah's oldest daughter Louisa Clark, age 17 or 18, married Squire McWorter, son of Frank. Louisa had obtained her freedom as a baby along with her 19-year-old mother Kesiah Clark in Kentucky in 1825. After Squire died in 1855, half the Clark family moved to Quincy where they continued as active abolitionists with others there, providing a destination for New Philadelphians accompanying freedom seekers headed north. (Terry and Claire Martin, 2010, page 87-88)

Simeon Clark, Louisa's brother, remarried after being widowed (with one son), and he and his second wife had three children by birth and adopted one more boy. By 1860 they and then-grandmother Kesiah lived in Quincy to the north of New Philadelphia where they were active conductors on the Underground Railroad, maintaining a passage for fugitives coming through New Philadelphia to the north. In 1870 he spoke to a large and integrated Quincy celebration of the end of slavery, recalling that he had "time and time again assisted his flying brothers from the pursuit of the negro-hunter and his bloodhounds."

Louisa Clark. Photo used with permission of the family; from the New Philadelphia Collection found in Newton, Kansas by descendant Conle White.

Simeon, Alexander, and Thomas Clark were among the younger generation that New Philadelphia relied upon as it grew. Alexander was a blacksmith in the town. Simeon and Alexander were likely born into slavery. According to the 1850 census, they and their siblings were born in Kentucky (2), Indiana, Virginia, Illinois (2), and finally Missouri. A saga of slavery and freedom, danger and safety, is buried in those moves from state to state but demonstrated in the closeness and strength of the three brothers, shown later in life in the photo here. Simeon at age 39 and Thomas at age 24 served one year together in Company F, United States Colored Troops 38th Regiment Infantry. They were part of the occupation of Richmond, Virginia in 1865. It was not until the North was unable to overcome the South that African Americans were finally permitted to enlist en masse. In many ways these soldiers won the war for the exhausted Union army.

Alexander Clark married Anna Jackson. They had three children: Mary Jane, Charles, and Emma. Charles perished at age 21; his gravestone reads "weep not Father and Mother for me, I will be waiting in Glory for thee." Anna probably died giving birth to

Left, Simeon Clark. Photo used with permission of the family; from the New Philadelphia Collection found in Newton, Kansas by descendant Conle White. **Right**, (left to right) Simeon, Alexander (standing), and Thomas Clark. Photo used with permission of the family; from the New Philadelphia Collection found in Newton, Kansas by descendant Conle White.

Emma, and Emma lived only to age two. But the Clarks pressed on, eventually migrating out of Illinois into Sedgwick County, Kansas, where family records and stories survive to today.

By the 1850s Jacob and Elizabeth Irick were farming about 3 miles southeast of New Philadelphia after Jacob bought 100 acres of his own father's military service bounty land. Five generations of Iricks shared work with McWorters and others at New Philadelphia, particularly the African American farmers. By working on each other's land when crops were ready to harvest or other tasks were pressing, everyone got their crops and livestock planted, grown, cared for, and to market or into storage for winter. Irick descendants still live near New Philadelphia and at least two have served on the board of the New Philadelphia Association, Harry Wright and David Iftner.

The Eckleberger family farmed just south of New Philadelphia from the 1800s into the 1900s, with children appearing in a 1925

Left, Anna and Mary Jane Jackson.
Photo used with permission of the family; from the New Philadelphia Collection found in Newton, Kansas by descendant Conle White.
Right, Charles Jackson. Photo courtesy of McWorter family.

New Philadelphia School photograph (see chapter 4).

The Eckelbergers were yet another example of multigenerational stability and engagement with the freedom struggle in and around New Philadelphia. Descendant Ruby Duke of Baylis told this story to Carrie Christman:

> When my momma was a little girl, she would go with my great-grandmother in an old buggy and go up the road to help deliver the little McWorter babies when they were born. The last one that was born there, my grandmother delivered it. It would be on her birth certificate. They'd have to truck produce and they'd haul them to the railroad to ship it out. When they would, they'd fill it with like crates of chickens or crates of produce. They had a box built under the bottom of the wagon and if a slave come in on the train, then they would hide them in it and take them back to the farm. When they would be working on my great-grandpa's farm, posses would come and try to find these runaway slaves. My mom

Top, Irick family. **Front row, left to right,** Anna Irick Saylor, Jacob Irick, Jr., Jacob Irick, Elizabeth Irick, William Irick, and Amanda Irick Reed. **Back row, left to right,** James Wesley Irick, Mary Jane Irick Troy, Andrew Irick, Laura Irick Harshman, and Jesse Irick. *Photo courtesy of Harry and Helen Wright.*
Bottom, Henry and Adeline Eckelberger. *Photo courtesy of the Eckelberger family.*

As with the Eckelberger's and their wagon, freedom seekers hid in the bottom of this wagon as they escaped. Only two such wagons from that perilous time are known to exist today, this one in North Carolina and one other belonging to Levi and Catherine Coffin in Indiana. Photo by Rebecca Lasley, used courtesy of Mendenhall Homeplace of Historic Jamestown Society, Inc., Jamestown, North Carolina.

had this great, big collie dog and they had it in their yard fenced in. Well, if these blacks would be there working for the great-grandparents, that dog would start barking at those posses coming up this little dirt lane to their house. If some of them that were out in the fields, they would take off and run to the creek. Down by the creek there was a big cave, which I already told someone about. The others would get in this box that was built under the nest where the chickens laid their eggs. Then, my grandparents would let a chicken out and that dog would kill the chicken. So, when the bounty hunters got there, that's what they thought was all the commotion. The dog was just killing a chicken. My great-grandpa never did lose one of the blacks then, even though they had a lot of people looking for them.

Ruby Duke also tells that her mother named her after a McWorter descendant named Ruby.

Due at least in part to the meaning and the achievements of New Philadelphia, the locale and its extended families kept a hold on people even as they migrated out. Numerous people who moved away are buried near New Philadelphia. Judy or Juda Armstead, Frank and Lucy's oldest daughter, married William Armstead when she was 53. Living almost to her 106th birthday, she outlived all her six siblings and lived most of her years as a free woman, unlike several of her siblings even though they were bought out of slavery at a younger age. She eventually settled in Jacksonville some 40 miles east; the household included her daughter and grandchildren as well as her niece Lucy Ann McWorter and Lucy Ann's husband George Brooks. Most of them were McWorters bought out of slavery by McWorters.

Juda's sister Lucy Ann McWorter is another daughter of Frank and Lucy who carried on the family freedom tradition. But before telling this next story, it is necessary to stop and point out that Frank's wife Lucy must have been respected, treasured and loved, because her children named five different granddaughters after her, either Lucy or Lucy Ann. These repeated names—not to mention the abundance of old thimbles in family collections and in the archaeology that was to come—are a precious trace of women's contributions to New Philadelphia. Too often we have to understand the women through their husband and families. So we consider the second Lucy in the family after her mother Free Lucy: Lucy Ann. Having arrived in New Philadelphia at age 6 with her parents, Lucy Ann married Ansel Vond from Parma, New York, near Rochester, in 1858. Like her, Ansel was the free son of a freed slave. By 1860 Ansel owned land next to Frank's farm and he and Lucy Ann had five children.

Rochester, New York was where Frederick Douglas lived and worked. Freedom was just across Lake Ontario in Canada, or westward down the coast in St. Catherine's, Ontario, where Harriet Tubman delivered her "passengers." Ansel's father lived in Parma long after escaping slavery himself. Ansel's oldest brother Walter stayed

Gravestone of Judy/Juda Armstead in New Philadelphia Cemetery. Photo by Claire Martin, used with permission.

there working his own boat as a fisherman selling to local restaurants. He is known to have rowed or sailed many people to freedom, moving either across the lake, down the coast, or to bigger boats waiting in deeper water. So Ansel settling in New Philadelphia, marrying a McWorter, participating in town lot purchases and sales as is documented, is precious evidence of the town's participation in the human network of freedom seekers and helpers that helped the United States throw off the bonds of slavery.

The obituary here relates that Ansel lived in New Philadelphia as long as he was able, relocating to live with offspring in Kansas, passing away soon with arrangements to transfer his body back for burial in New Philadelphia.

Again with the help of Terry and Claire Martin (2010, page 92), we can trace the story of another migrant from Western New York state, the European-American Arden B. Cobb, born in Steuben County 1830.

Left, Lucy Ann McWorter Vond, of New Philadelphia, Illinois. Photo courtesy of the McWorter family.

Right, This last known picture taken of Ansel Vond includes four generations. Next to him is his daughter Lucy Vond Thomas, holding her grandson Reginald Watts. Standing behind Lucy is Ansel's granddaughter and Reginald's mother Annie Thomas Watts. Standing behind Ansel is his granddaughter Marie Thomas. Photo courtesy of Lonie Wilson.

The Cobb family emigrated to Perry Township, Pike County, Illinois around 1843, and the young Arden began learning the harness and saddle-making trade. He practiced his first trade for about six years in Perry Township, until shortly after his marriage to Emily J. Shields in 1852 (USBC 1850a; Chapman 1880:631; ISAISGS 1990).

Cobb began to study medicine with a local physician in the early 1850s. In 1856 and 1857 he attended a medical college in Missouri. He returned to Pike County, purchased the lots in New Philadelphia, and began practicing medicine. Arden and Emily Cobb and their five children lived in New Phila-

DEATH OF ANSEL VOND

Was a Pioneer in Illinois and Later in Oklahoma

Ansel Vond, 86 years old, died last night at six o'clock at the home of his son-in-law, Mr. William Thomas at 321 Missouri street. Mr. Vond pioneered in Illinois and later in Oklahoma and had been living in Lawrence only since the first of the year.

The body will be shipped to the old home in Pike County, Ill., today and will be accompanied by his daughter and son-in-law, who will return to Lawrence after the funeral.

Obituary of Ansel Vond, Lawrence Daily Journal-World, September 11, 1915. Photo courtesy of Kansas Historical Society.

delphia until Emily's death in 1868. Cobb served as postmaster for four years, as school director, and as justice of the peace (Hadley Township 1855–1882:24,27; Chapman 1880:631).

Many of the photographs from the town of New Philadelphia were taken in the studio of Burnham Photography in Barry, Illinois, including several of those here. The subjects appear as strong people rooted in the land of the Midwest frontier: 19th century farm families probably dressed in their Sunday best for the photographer. In some cases their attire is unpretentious. Others wear the latest fashion from St. Louis, Chicago or the East Coast. The town was small but not isolated. Among all the images, there is no known photograph of the town founder and hero of New Philadelphia, Frank McWorter.

Top, Julia McWorter Coleman, Solomon's daughter and Free Frank and Lucy's granddaughter. *Right*, Unidentified man, New Philadelphia. Both photos courtesy of the McWorter family and the New Philadelphia Collection found in Newton, Kansas by descendant Conle White.

Top, Unidentified man, New Philadelphia.
Right, Unidentified men, New Philadelphia. Both photos courtesy of the McWorter family and the New Philadelphia Collection found in Newton, Kansas by descendant Conle White.

Top left, Unidentified woman and young man, New Philadelphia.
Top right, Unidentified man and woman, New Philadelphia. Photo courtesy of the McWorter family and the New Philadelphia Collection found in Newton, Kansas by descendant Conle White.
Bottom, Unidentified man, New Philadelphia. All three photos courtesy of the McWorter family and the New Philadelphia Collection found in Newton, Kansas by descendant Conle White.

Chapter Four

Settlement

After the end of New Philadelphia's formal status as a town in 1885, it persisted as an informal settlement. People continued to live in and around the town site. Children up to the 8th grade attended New Philadelphia School until the year 1947-1948 when many one-room schoolhouses in the county were closed and children started attending bigger schools in nearby towns, just as high school students had done for decades.

Just as New Philadelphia lost official recognition as a town, industrialization was accelerating nationwide, pulling people into the cities and pushing them off the farms. This was true across Pike County; the U.S. Census records its population peaking in 1880. But New Philadelphia had already figured into an additional drama, that of the coming of the railroad in 1869.

Hannibal and Naples Railroad Company set out to connect Hannibal, Missouri to Naples, Illinois through Phillips Ferry, later called Valley City, Illinois. Rather than taking the straight line from the higher elevation west to the lower elevation east, the rail line detoured around New Philadelphia when it was completed. Various histories report that the town declined after missing out on the opportunity to become a stop on the railroad, with the commerce that brings. The railroad investors were Missourians. Missouri was until 1865 a slave state. What happened?

Recent research by Christopher Fennell pieces together the story. Without leaving us a single bit of official evidence, the company made a decision to avoid New Philadelphia. In fact, the surviving archives of the railway and its subsequent owners do not even mention the town, although they do mention other places and features along the route.

The detour to the north cost the company money. It involved longer distance and therefore more track and more time to build and travel. It involved a curve, which put wear and tear on the track. It involved climbing and then descending, so much that larger trains needed a helper engine (and the labor and time that entailed) to help pull them up the incline. It did not avoid any difficult terrain or water.

The railroad did not pass through any other town by detouring, although a small town later sprung up at Baylis, where the train stopped near New Philadelphia. There were no large landholders who might have lobbied for the detour, with the possible exception of the farmer John McTucker, who served the railroad company as local liaison. He died in 1869 and his heirs ended up with a small train stop on that land. But they did not develop that farm into a town.

Moreover, the Walker and McWorter families each gave permission to the railroad company to traverse their farmland, as farmers generally did. In any case, the detour was built in, and the town soon became a rural settlement. Decades later the railroad line was actually moved to straighten out the detour, but the town and even the settlement had dwindled by then.

In spite of this drama of local elites, the people who stayed in the area carried on with their lives. The *Barry Adage* reported in June 1873 that Solomon McWorter drove "100 fat cattle" to the Barry train depot to ship them to Buffalo, New York. If we could talk with him as the train pulled out carrying his livestock, he could certainly tell us the whole story.

Remembering early 20th century New Philadelphia, local historian and journalist Grace Matteson wrote, "At the schoolhouse many annual fairs were held. With contests. Races, exhibitions of home arts and all the things that go with a fair." The community lived on through rituals of Midwest culture of those times. For some aspects

Percent of US labor force in farming	
1790	90%
1840	69%
1880	49%
1920	27%
1960	8%
2000	2%

By 2000, farming only employed one in 50 U.S. workers. Data from Spielmaker, 2005.

of economy and society, New Philadelphia families joined the people of Barry, Illinois, just 4 miles west, as they had to a lesser degree in the 19th century.

Both African Americans and European Americans lived in the settlement of New Philadelphia. Families sent young men to fight in World Wars I and II. Inside New Philadelphia they tended to experience integration, but outside they tended to experience segregation, for example in the military.

The settlement was based on a rural agricultural experience. Family life was the priority because a strong and large family was the basis for economic survival, running successful farms with family labor. The scourge of alcoholism was a threat to this, so it was logical that New Philadelphians invited Carrie Nation to come and lecture. Her visit and talk was a big event, remembered long after.

Work was disappearing—in part due to the machinery adopted on the farms—but social ties were strong. These ties brought back relatives and friends who had moved out for survival, mostly to cities. Some came to family reunions or community events. Others just came to visit, sometimes with a little homesickness. Over time the rural population in the United States shrunk to just one in 5 people. So, along with seeing friends and family there was also a pull to get

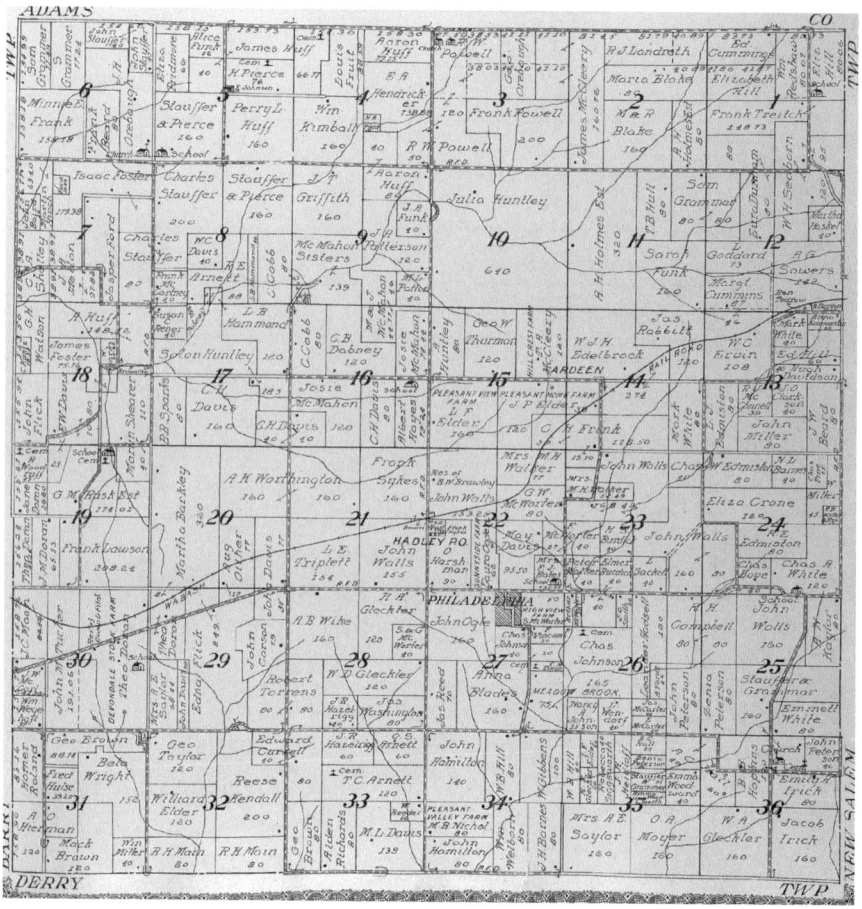

Plat map of New Philadelphia, ca. 1912. Photo from Standard Atlas of Pike County, 1912; public domain.

out of the city for a bit, back on the farm, and even show your children how life used to be and where they came from. The settlement was no longer a town, but it did have wider connections. And these connections may have become more fragile, but they were deeply felt.

This plat map here shows how farmed and settled the land around New Philadelphia was by 1912. Each quarter of each numbered section is about 160 acres, so there are numerous households with much smaller farms, particularly close to New Philadelphia and

Left, The settlement of New Philadelphia and surrounding farms in the 1930s. Aero Service Corp., 1936. Public domain.
Right, The settlement of New Philadelphia in the 1960s. Park Aerial Surveys, Inc., 1968. Public domain.

along the east-west road north of the settlement that was the main route between the Mississippi and the Illinois before the railroads were built.

A photo taken in 1932 as part of a statewide aerial survey provides insight into the evolution from town to settlement. A square area can be seen, which residents called the Park, that gave special structure and shared common space to the six households in the former town. Eight more houses, also with outbuildings suggesting shelter for farm equipment, livestock and supplies, are visible in the close environs. Notice the dotted areas; these are quite likely apple orchards, which was a major market crop in the area. The map shows lots of paths and irregularities from slopes and small creeks and gulleys; that geography indicates that a variety of crops and livestock were being raised.

Around thirty years later Illinois carried out another statewide aerial survey, yielding another photo of the settlement. Many changes are visible in this 1960s detail of New Philadelphia. The Park is gone. We see only four house-outbuilding complexes and one lone house or other building to the north. The orchards have been replaced by grain crops of some kind, which are farmed with more

Top, New Philadelphia farmer harvesting grain with a team of three massive horses pulling the cutting tool. Photo courtesy of the McWorter family.
Middle, A team of people, horses, and machines harvesting wheat. Photo courtesy of the McWorter family.
Bottom, An Advance Rumely threshing machine. Photo courtesy of the McWorter family.

Top, Rumely Oil Pull tractor. Photo courtesy of the McWorter family. *Bottom*, Farm work going on near the barn and chicken coop then belonging to the Burdick family, located on the townsite of New Philadelphia. Photo courtesy of the McWorter family.

machinery and less human power. Production for use has waned; production for market is more dominant. The contour of the land is changed, smoothed by the tractors that have crisscrossed it.

As New Philadelphia went from being a town to a settlement, both crops and the methods of farming underwent change. Early agricultural activity was powered by human and animal. Once the crop was bound up in what are called sheaves, several sheaves were

Food stall outside New Philadelphia School on July 4. Photo courtesy of the McWorter family.

set up to lean against each other. That kept them from rotting and helped them dry in the sun and wind.

Over time, machines assumed a greater role. Horses continued to provide power, but now that power was supplementary. One photo shows a tractor turning a belt that is attached to an Advance Rumely threshing machine. In this way the tractor activates the threshing process that separates the grain—typically oats or wheat—from the rest of the plant. The horses pull the harvested plants to the machine and men throw the bundles into the thresher. Whoever isn't lifting bundles is watching closely to keep everything moving smoothly and safely. The additional capacity provided by machines did not entirely supplant older communal labor practices, and according to stories from many local families, African Americans and European Americans worked on each other's farms as needed.

The kerosene-powered Rumely Oil Pull tractor was only manufactured between 1910 and 1930 in Laporte, Indiana. New Philadelphia farmers were known to have up-to-date technology, and at least one young McWorter—Festus, the son of Arthur and grandson of Solomon—kept his subscription to *Farm Journal* long after he'd left the farm and moved to Chicago.

Close up of food stall, New Philadelphia School. Photo courtesy of the McWorter family.

The combination of forces it took to grow food and raise animals is represented in the photo here of people, equipment, a fruit tree, the chicken coop in front, and the all-important barn. In January 2017 at least one chicken was laying eggs there.

Just as food production was a shared task, so was food appreciation and consumption. The New Philadelphia School was the site of many events besides school, as the photo here shows. Holidays were the occasion for community gatherings and cultural activities. Food growers, visitors, and perhaps even event judges or officials are there to explain, admire, and critique.

At the center of most celebrations in all farming communities is the displaying and admiring of produce and livestock. The back of the stall in the previous photos shows apples (probably multiple varieties), peppers, potatoes, various stone fruit, grapes, tomatoes, a pumpkin, and an unusual gourd, as well as a whole shelf of large

Top, Back of food stall, New Philadelphia School.
Bottom, Chickens and turkeys with the farmer and onlookers. Photos courtesy of the McWorter family.

canned (that is to say, bottled) produce to eat through the winter, and small jars of jam. The 42-star flags on this stall indicate this is most likely July 4, 1890. The new state of Idaho had been admitted to the union just the day before, so the 43-star flag was not yet on

Left to right, Siblings Cordell, Ellen, Thelma, Festus and cousin William McWorter with their Hampshire pigs. Photo courtesy of the McWorter family.

the market.

There is a tradition of poultry farming in the New Philadelphia area that continues to the present day. According to family lore, one New Philadelphia family raised white turkeys and another raised white ducks, both unique in the local area. That meant that any birds that "flew the coop" could be reunited with their owner without a squabble.

The raising of livestock was another agricultural activity in New Philadelphia. The photo shows descendant children of Frank McWorter, the town founder, with their Hampshire pigs. Their body language communicates expertise and confidence with animal husbandry. Arthur McWorter registered the perigree of at least some of his pigs. Maybe Lady Pike, whose sire and dam were bred by Willie Essig and Albert Oitker, is in this photo with the young farmers.

Apple packing was a major industry of the area during the first half of the 20th century. In the photo here is shown LeMoyne Washington, the last African American descendant of New Philadelphia to live in the area. Third from right is Jacob Iftner, who was descend-

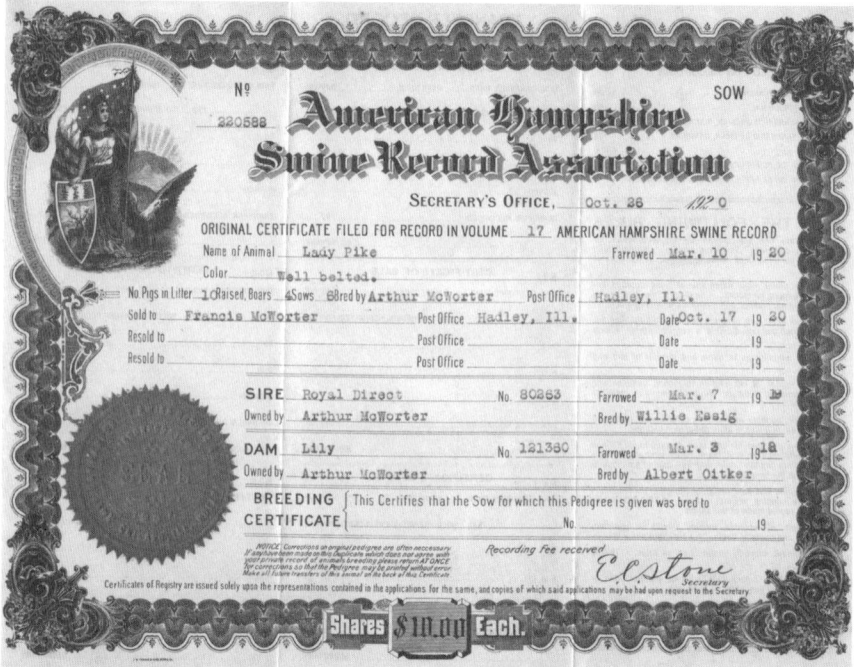

Top, One of several such documents still in the family, Arthur McWorter obtained this certified breeding record for a Hampshire pig named Lady Pike. Image courtesy of the McWorter family.

Bottom, Workers in apple processing shed, Barry, Illinois. LeMoyne Washington is second from right, Jacob Iftner is third from right. Photo courtesy of Stroemer Foods, Barry, Illinois.

Top, This undated portrait of New Philadelphia school includes three Butler sisters: Irene in the white dress next to end in top row, Dora with her head in the doorway, and Golden just below Dora. Photo courtesy of Ron Carter.

Right, Schoolhouse, New Philadelphia. Photo courtesy of New Philadelphia Association.

ed from the Iricks who are shown in chapter 3. Jacob's nephew Harry Wright, longtime U of I extension agent and Pike county board member, co-founded the New Philadelphia Association and continues to serve to this day. The photo hangs with others in Stroemer's, the grocery store in Barry, Illinois.

Top, New Philadelphia school students Gerald Arnett, Lillie Booth, Alvin Burdick, Everett Gibson, Pearl Gibson, Neal Gibson, Naomi Gibson, Lloyd Gibson, Erma Hull, Ellen McWorter, Cora Siefers, Geneva Venicombe, Manford Venicombe, Leonard Venicombe, Frankie Venicombe, and Ernest Venicombe, and teacher Carrie Glasgow ca. 1917.
Left, Carrie Glasgow, teacher, New Philadelphia School.
Photos courtesy of Mary Kay Arnett.

Until 1947, elementary education in the county took place in one-room schoolhouses that students could walk to more easily than today's countywide elementary schools. The one-room New Philadelphia School was built on Frank McWorter's original farm, the land and funds for supplies donated by the family. Students worked at various grade levels up to 8th grade guided by one teacher. Built

A 1919 or 1920 snapshot of New Philadelphia school students. **Front row, left to right,** *Gladys McWorter, Margaret and Lloyd Gibson, Ellen McWorter, Grace Nichols, Festus McWorter.* **Back row,** *Gerald Arnett, Alvin Burdick, Naomi Gibson, Cofa Siefers, Vivian Eckelberger, Lilllie Booth, Louise Eckelberger. Photo courtesy of Russell Gibson.*

in 1874 and used until 1947 or 1948, the school was just across the road north from the former town of New Philadelphia. Class size over the decades, as shown here, reflects the nationwide migration to the cities.

New Philadelphia schoolteacher Carrie Glasgow gave a small autograph book to third grader Gerald Arnett and his family kept it safe for 100 years. The two photos here were pasted in the book. The students were also listed, and counting the last names suggests that at least seven families sent their children to the New Phila-

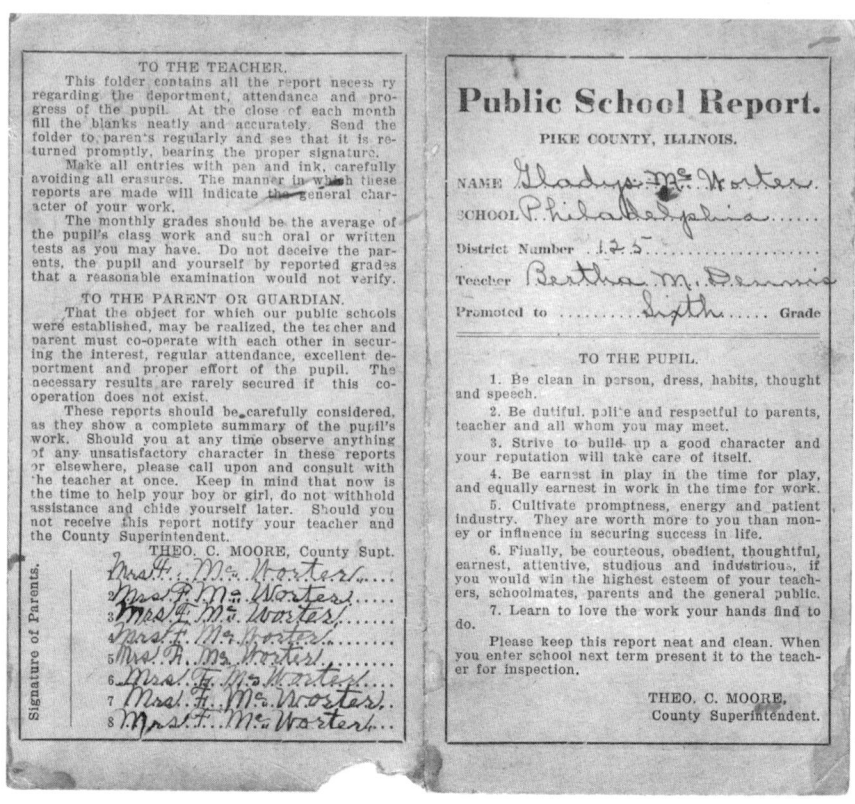

Sixth-grade report card of Gladys McWorter from New Philadelphia School in 1922. Its seven goals for the student are an example of Pike County moral education of the time. Photo courtesy of the McWorter family.

delphia school that year. The photos came from the Arnett family, which still owns some New Philadelphia land. The Arnetts are also descended from the Iricks.

Judging from the last names, at least eight families sent their children to school in 1917, and there was some continuity over the eight years from 1917 to 1925. Two students in the 1925 class, Louise and Marjorie Eckelberger, were grandchildren of Henry and Adeline Eckelberger, whose story is told in chapter 3.

Shaw School was two miles from New Philadelphia School. The photo here with its precious names indicates that 15 families sent 37 children to Shaw in 1896. The 1925 photo shows 14 students from

Top, New Philadelphia School, 1925. **Seated left to right,** *Hazel Johnson, Naomi Marley, Edna Stillflew, Ruby Bowen, Pauline Eckelberger, and Marjorie Eckelberger.* **Middle row left to right,** *Helen Eckleberger, two unidentified girls, Gladys McWorter, Margaret Gibson, Louise Eckleberger, Mildred Stillflew.* **Back row left to right,** *teacher Fay Bennet, Harry Johnson, Paul Burdick, Lloyd Gibson, Festus McWorter, Cordell McWorter, unidentified boy, Wayne Johnson. Photo courtesy of the McWorter family; names courtesy of Wilma Waters, from* Pike County Illinois Schools, 1832–1995.

nine families. The careful photo- and name-keeping reflects a measure of family stability as well as respect for earlier generations and what they accomplished.

Since farming depended on a strong families who could work hard, at least some New Philadelphians embraced abstinence from alcohol. In the 1890s they invited Carrie Nation to speak at nearby Shaw School, shown here. According to one account, "It was one

Top of page 116, New Philadelphia School students in 1927. Left to right, seated: Paul Burdick, Ernest Venicombe, Naomi Gibson, Floyd Kellum, Pauline Eckelberger. Middle row: Hazel Johnson, Cordell McWorter, Harry Johnson, Dee Kellum, Festus McWorter, Marjorie Eckelberger, Wayne Johnson. Back row: Lloyd Gibson, Helen Kellum, Claude and Clyde Preston, Ellen or Bernice McWorter, Gladys McWorter. Photo submitted by Gerald Kellum to Pike Press, used with permission.

Bottom of page 116, Shaw School, two miles away from New Philadelphia School. Photo from Pike County Illinois Schools, *published by the Pike County Historical Society, used with permission.*

Top, As the slate board indicates, this photo of Shaw School students and their teacher was taken on October 28, 1896. **First row left to right,** Georgie Coulter, Frank Nichol, Charles Washington, Walter Nichol, Roy Hazelrigg, Floyd Nichol, Marion Richards, Willie Welbourne, Jim Coulter, Raymond Kendall. Second row: Maggie Payne, Bell Payne, Anna Coulter, (unknown) Moyer, Nettie Nichol, Clara Richards, Mary Richards, Mamie Rhodes, Lena Hadsell, Goldie Moyer, Velma Arnett. **Back row:** Bell Washington, Ada Washington, Fannie Arnett, Anna Richards, Minnie Dolbeare, Bell Hazelrigg, teacher Fan Robb, Millie Arnett, Willie Kerr, Edna Dolbeare, Fred Auer, Golden Welbourne, Robert Richards, Robert Nichol, Alpha Welbourne, Edd Hazelrigg, and Arnie (or possibly Chris) Payne. Photo courtesy of Rebecca Watson Acuff.

Top, Shaw School students and teacher, 1925. **Front row left to right,** Robert Gleckler, Wathena Hazelbrigg, Mary Jo Cooley (Baughman) (back of photo says Berdalla Clowers), Betty McPherson, Mary Dell Zircle, James Washington, Juanita Washington. **Back row left to right,** teacher Elden Fesler, Lloyd Nichol, Harold Harris, Lawrence Alexander, Marjorie Washington, Ruby Jean Washington, Charles Edward Washington, Alden Hazelrigg. Photo courtesy of Roma McConnell Weir, from Pike County Natives 1999.
Left, Carrie Nation. Portrait photo public domain via Wikimedia.

Sunday school group in front of either the New Philadelphia or Shaw schoolhouse. Photo courtesy of the McWorter family.

of the most noteworthy meetings ever held at Shaw School," (Pike County Natives et al., 1999, page 78) and the story of that day was passed down to modern descendants. Carrie used a hatchet when she entered bars to break liquor bottles, and lectured nationwide, selling souvenir hatchets. Arthur McWorter (see photo) was among the organizers of this event as a young man in his 20s.

Some New Philadelphians attended churches in the larger town of Barry, which were Baptist or Methodist. But religious services in New Philadelphia were nondenominational, and were held in the schoolhouse.

Despite the "country mile" that often separated each farmhouse, the families of the New Philadelphia settlement were close friends. The families shared in work, play, and cultural activities; for example, they would eat together during the warmer months, a sure sign that strong community ties existed in the area.

Arthur McWorter (1874–1950) married Ophelia Walker (1883–1914). Both were born in New Philadelphia and lived their lives there. Arthur was the last McWorter to farm the land in the New Philadelphia settlement before retiring to Chicago to live with his

Top left, New Philadelphia residents eating together.
Top right, Two friends on a horse in 1918: Cordell McWorter in back and Virgil Burdick in front.
Bottom left, Arthur McWorter.
Bottom right, Ophelia Walker McWorter.
Photos courtesy of the McWorter family.

Seated, left to right, Cordell and Festus; Standing, left to right, Bernice, Thelma, and Ellen McWorter. Photo courtesy of the McWorter family.

children. Ophelia died very early, and then Arthur moved into the house that had first been his grandfather Frank McWorter's, then his father Solomon's. Arthur and his mother Frances Jane Coleman McWorter raised the five children.

Thelma (1906-2001), Ellen (1911-1989), Festus (1912-2008), Bernice (1912-1997), and Cordell (1914-1987), the children of Arthur and Ophelia Walker McWorter, and Alberta (1902-2008) and Gladys (1912-1987), the children of Francis and Sadie McWorter, were among the last of the old families to be born and raised in New Philadelphia. They migrated to big cities as adults, but returned repeatedly to maintain relationships with neighbors and classmates.

Francis McWorter (1872–1949) and Sadie Walker McWorter (1875–unknown), both born in New Philadelphia, were married October 27, 1898. In the photo here they are celebrating their 50th wedding anniversary. They lived and farmed across the road from New

This early 1920s gathering at New Philadelphia included the family names Butler, McWorter, Walker, Washington, and Zimmerman. Names were written on the back of the photo to identify each person. **Front row, left to right,** William McWorter (J. E.'s son), Gladys McWorter, Cordell McWorter, Ellen McWorter, and Festus McWorter. **Middle row, left to right,** Margaret Johnson Walker, Frances Jane Coleman McWorter, and Mary, for whom no last name was written. **Back row, left to right,** Hermes Zimmerman, Alberta McWorter, Francis McWorter, Sadie McWorter, Mr. William Butler, John McWorter, Stella Zimmerman, Mr. Washington, Charlotte (Mrs. George) McWorter, Albert Walker, Arthur McWorter, George McWorter. Hermes Zimmerman was a stepson of Charlotte McWorter (from the 1920 census) and (from ancestry.com) was the corresponding secretary of the Race Friendship League at the Garrett Theological Seminary on the campus of Northwestern where he was evidently a student, according to a 1925 yearbook. He was later a minister in Beloit, Wisconsin. Stella Zimmerman was a stepdaughter of Charlotte McWorter. Photo courtesy of the McWorter family.

Left, Two women, New Philadelphia. One is a Butler, related to William Butler in the previous photo.
Right, left to right, Will McWorter and Alex Clark were neighbors and first cousins in the New Philadelphia settlement.
Bottom, Francis McWorter and Sadie Walker McWorter on the occasion of their 50th wedding anniversary. Photos courtesy of the McWorter family.

Philadelphia until their passing. Two daughters, Alberta and Gladys (whose report card is reproduced here) attended New Philadelphia School and then Barry High School.

Charles Washington and brothers Thomas and Shelby McWorter were three African Americans from New Philadelphia who served in the armed forces in World War I, each registering in 1917. Shelby registered in Pike County and Thomas registered in Montana, where he had found work. Thomas registered as white on his draft card,

Left, Thomas and Shelby McWorter.
Right, Charles Washington. Photos from With the Colors in Pike County, Illinois; *Public domain.*

although the clerk made his own note: "Negro descent." Twenty-five years later, on April 26, 1942, Thomas registered for World War II in Las Vegas and Shelby in Los Angeles. They each declared "white" on their draft cards. The Depression years and the search for employment in a racist society were probably the biggest factors in this. Although their family history was a secret from their offspring, living descendants remember details of their lives that give clues to Thomas's and Shelby's disconnect from family and heritage.

The house built by Frank McWorter on his farm served as the home for four generations. It stood across the main road from the platted streets of New Philadelphia proper. In the first photo, the "safety bicycle" (which meant having two equal size wheels) helps to date the photo as 1880s or later, for it came into use then. In the next picture, the woman's big "leg of mutton" sleeves date the photo to between the 1890s and roughly 1905. According to Thelma McWorter's handwriting on back, this was taken "at the Frances Jane Coleman McWorter Bates home in Hadley, IL." When New Philadelphia ceased to be an official town, everyone's address become Hadley and

Top, Family members at Frank McWorter home, ca. 1880s or later.
Bottom, Family members at Frank McWorter home, ca. 1890s to 1905.
Left to right, Arthur McWorter, Lucy, (Frances) Jane, and a cousin.
Photos courtesy of the McWorter family.

Top left, *Uncles stand near nephews in this family portrait in front of the Frank McWorter house.* **Left to right:** *John, Festus, and Cordell McWorter, Frances Jane Coleman McWorter Bates, Thelma, William, and Arthur McWorter. Photo courtesy of the McWorter family.*
Top and middle right photos, *two views of the first Burdick House.*
Bottom, *Second Burdick house, into which the Burdicks moved in 1942 and lived until 1982, eventually selling it to the New Philadelphia Association. First Burdick house is on the right. The Burdicks farmed in New Philadelphia for more than 100 years. Burdick House photos courtesy of Ruth Burdick.*

Top left, Second Burdick house, interior. Photo courtesy of Ruth Burdick.
Top right, Virgil Burdick's 1942 house with working outbuildings, ca. 1955. Photo from Drury 1955.
Bottom left, Ellsworth Burdick's house and farm, just to the south of his father Virgil's farm. Ellsworth's dairy barn indicates that the farm was used at that time or earlier for milk cows. Photo from Drury 1955.
Bottom right, Cordell McWorter and Neil Gibson, Barry High School reunion. Cordell was a New Philadelphian who returned at intervals to see old friends and places. Photo courtesy of the McWorter family.

even later Barry. The third photo is taken a bit later and so the next generation appears in greater numbers.

Thelma McWorter returned to New Philadelphia on many occasions. Thelma also painted New Philadelphia at least twice. In the painting on page 129, the Frank McWorter farm just north of the town with its five tall front windows is the largest white building at the bottom. New Philadelphia School is just to the right, on his land but situated on the corner which was ideal for produce displays. Across the road at bottom right in the painting is Francis and Sadie

Left, Unidentified man and woman, New Philadelphia. The settlement continued to maintain its ties with the larger world, as evidenced by the combination of urban and rural styles in this New Philadelphian's hat and overalls.

Right, Unidentified woman, New Philadelphia. Another example of urban and rural intersecting, as the woman's fur trimmed coat and the barn reflect how people were bridging distant city life and the old familiarity of rural Pike County. Photos courtesy of the McWorter family.

McWorter's farm. Thelma painted the roads, houses, barns, water pumps, crops in the fields, an apple orchard, and the railroad. In a rural setting, trains could be heard even from far away. They were important to the local economy, and the particular story of trains and New Philadelphia may have been passed down to her. A variety of children told stories of stopping by Francis and Sadie McWorter's house on the way home from school on very cold days and getting warmed up and cheered on their way, if not driven all the way home.

On September 16, 1963 LeMoyne Washington sat on the bench in the photo on page 130 or one near it in Lafayette Park in Barry, Illinois, not five miles from New Philadelphia where he was born and raised. It was the time of Black people's active struggle to end apartheid-like conditions of segregation and to be able to vote. It was also one day after four racists had bombed the 16th Street Baptist

Painting of New Philadelphia by Thelma McWorter. Photo by Jaclyn Nash.

Church in Birmingham, Alabama, killing 4 little African American girls as they put on their choir robes, 2 teenage boys, and injuring 22 others. Harry Wright, a local descendant of Jacob Irick who had helped farm New Philadelphia 100 years earlier asked LeMoyne what he was doing sitting there, and he told Harry, "I'm sitting here protesting America." As local genealogist Kathy Robinson tells it, "LeMoyne Washington lived with my folks down in Pleasant Hill before he died. I like the fact that LeMoyne had cared for Virgil Burdick in Virgil's old age and when LeMoyne needed help, Virgil's granddaughter-in-law, Mary Burdick-Robinson (my step-mom), took care of LeMoyne. Isn't that the way it's supposed to work?"

Top, This 1979 photo brings together Cordell McWorter of Chicago with LeMoyne Washington of Barry. Photo courtesy of the McWorter family. **Bottom,** Bench, Lafayette Park, Barry, Illinois. Photo by Kate Williams-McWorter.

Chapter Five

Memory

Memory in a general sense is about the ability to remember. There are at least four institutional resources that are the usual basis for expanding our individual capacity to remember. Each of these arose to look after the collective good in society. In fact memory is the basis for culture and the preservation of our social relations, it is the foundation of our identity. The four main institutions of memory are the following:

1. Government records – This is especially true at the county level, as every county has a courthouse that usually contains the documents of marriage, life and death, and property transactions. At the national level there are the census records, the National Archives, and the Library of Congress. A special source for the national memory is the Congressional Record, as well as the research libraries set up for documenting every presidential administration.
2. Media archives – Newspapers and magazines exist at the national, regional, state, and local levels. They are increasingly being digitized, making available detailed information about the details of social life across the decades of the last several centuries.
3. Community institutions – At the community level the universal memory institutions are the libraries and schools, with the reference librarian the usual point of contact. Museums are special institution that preserve and display the material artifacts of history. Other community institutions, frequently

keep archives too: churches, social clubs, even special annual events.
4. Families – Through scrapbooks, entries in family Bibles, collections of correspondence, and the archives of individual lives. Some family members develop genealogical documentation so that they can share a narrative of family experience across the generations.

Even when the settlement of New Philadelphia returned to farmland, it was remembered. More than that, it was in people's hearts as a vision of what was possible for the entire country: a diverse community of African Americans and European Americans who could cooperate as friends and neighbors. The last residents of the town lots, the Burdicks, left in the 1980s, but some descendants of the town and the settlement continued to live in Pike County. The last members of the old families who grew up in or near New Philadelphia were born before World War II and are few in number today, but their descendants are living into the 21st century. Relying on the four kinds of memory institutions above, the place and the feats of its founders and residents were put into print; museums and other institutions protected and shared artifacts and documents that helped people remember; and families told stories, sometimes pulling out precious photographs and papers. Key books were published and even reprinted.

Why was it remembered through the decades? Why was New Philadelphia history kept alive? Because it was a unique story, for the people in Pike County and beyond. The McWorters were the first non-Native American family to settle in Hadley Township in Pike County. As more settlers came, they were a Black family in a mainly white environment, a family who provided leadership for everyone. They were joined by others like them. One aspect of leadership was economic, as owners of land and the developers of the town of New Philadelphia. Another aspect was religious. Frank and Lucy were leading members of the First Baptist Church of Barry, Illinois, as documented in church records. Most important of all was their leadership in the politics of freedom. Freedom was the motivation for

Left to right, 1975 Barry Apple Festival Parade participants James Walker, Darlene Kirkpatrick, Lisa Hunter, Cordell McWorter, Thelma McWorter Kirkpatrick Wheaton. Photo courtesy of the McWorter family.

everything the family did and this became the character of the town they established. This included not only freedom for themselves, but for others. This story was always known and frequently written about.

The McWorter family was known for their neighborliness and being strong advocates of community solidarity. The last McWorter residing in the area was William LeMoyne Washington, or Lee, who lived in Barry, Illinois until his death in 1998. He was well-known and admired in the area. Pike County was known for its apple orchards, and a photo of LeMoyne with Jacob Irick and others packing apples (page 110, bottom) hangs in Barry's only grocery store. One year he was Grand Marshall of the annual Apple Festival Parade. This parade is also an example of how cultural performance can be a vehicle for community memory.

    How was New Philadelphia remembered? The record of the town and the later settlement was always available to anyone interested in finding it. Local historians were aware of the story of New Philadelphia, with the first lengthy and detailed writing on the subject being Grace Matteson's 1964 booklet (page 138, right). The archives of the Pike County Courthouse has always held the historical records concerning property and family in New Philadelphia, as all the nation's county courthouses do for their residents. Local newspapers as well as the nation's leading African American newspaper the *Chicago Defender* had reported about life in New Philadelphia: Sunday school, family social events, economic activities, even individuals as they traveled throughout the region. The *Defender's* record contains the memory of the Black experience in the city, the state, and the entire country. Not only were these stories archived, they were quoted in modern media. Those county history compilations were another source that included the story and the people of New Philadelphia. Not all of them did, which illustrates how New Philadelphia was not always in the official narrative of Illinois or the nation.

    The Barry Historical Museum and its second curator Janita Metcalf kept and displayed clippings and photographs, unearthing more records along the way. Metcalf, also the archivist of the First Baptist Church of Barry, was a storehouse of knowledge and played a key role in documenting the relationship of Frank and New Philadelphia with the town of Barry. With Janita having gathered many family histories, the third museum curator Dee Forshey along with Janet Treadwell and others on the museum board were able to publish the latest local history in 2016, *Barry Family Histories,* and are now focused on raising funds to conserve the Civil War flag in the museum. Many of these different people are partners and collaborators. Janita and her husband

Janita Metcalf (1924–2014), second curator or director of the Barry Historical Museum. Photo by Kate Williams-McWorter.

led the Apple Festival Parade that featured Thelma Elise McWorter Kirkpatrick Wheaton and other descendants on a float representing the Frank and Lucy McWorters and their children. The farmer Larry Armistead, who eventually owned much of the New Philadelphia land, imagined the stories many times with his wife Natalie.

In addition, descendants have deposited material in other memory institutions: the Barry Public Library; The Abraham Lincoln Presidential Library in Springfield, Illinois; the DuSable Museum of African American History in Chicago; the Chicago Historical Society; and two Smithsonian Institutions, the National Museum of African American History and the National Museum of American History. Descendants and others took inspiration from what they

Their Ancestor Founded a Pike County Town

SPECIAL GUESTS at the Pike County Historical Society meeting April 13 were some of the descendants of "Free Frank" McWorter whose history was the subject for the evening's program. In this group are, left to right, top row: Cordell McWorter of Maywood and his daughter Patricia, great-grandson and great-great-granddaughter of Free Frank; Mrs Alberta McWorter Ewing of Chicago, great-granddaughter of Free Frank; Mrs Elizabeth Reeves of Jacksonville, granddaughter of Wm. Butler, early settler of New Philadelphia, the town laid out by Free Frank in Hadley township; Mrs Mattie Blue of Jacksonville, a friend; Bottom row: Mrs Nellie Le— of Pittsfield, a friend; Mrs Irene Butler Brown Jacksonville, mother of Mrs Reeves and daughter Wm. Butler; Thelma McWorter Kirkpatrick of cago, great-granddaughter of Free Frank. The wor are displaying some of the family documents and etching of Free Frank's wife, Lucy. Lemoyne W ington of Barry, grandson of James Washington wl second wife was the granddaughter of Free Fra had left for home when this photo was taken. story Page 4, Section B). —Republican Staff P

Article in the Pike County Republican *on a Pike County Historical Society evening program about New Philadelphia in 1977. Descendants and friends, including LeMoyne Washington (who was noted as having "left before the photo was taken") were special guests.* **Standing, left to right,** *Cordell McWorter and his daughter Patricia; Alberta McWorter Ewing; Elizabeth Reeves, granddaughter of William Butler; and a friend, Mattie Blue.* **Seated, left to right,** *a friend Nellie Le--; Irene Butler Brown, mother of Elizabeth and daughter of William Butler; and Thelma McWorter. At front are the displays they brought of relevant historical documents. Photo courtesy of Janita Metcalf.*

A crew of linotype workers create the lines of type that will become the Chicago Defender. *Until these machines were invented, most papers were eight pages or less, because it was so costly and time-consuming to arrange the metal type one letter at a time. Photo by Farm Security Administration. Public domain via Wikimedia Commons.*

knew, could learn, and could see in their family archives. For example, documents about New Philadelphia just recently arrived for this book project from Kensington, Minnesota; Hilo, Hawaii; and the Winterthur Museum and Library in Philadelphia, Pennsylvania. These widely dispersed documents are letters written in the 1800s by Clarissa Shipman, a neighbor and friend of Frank and Lucy and their children. Above all, a few highly valued individuals published about New Philadelphia through the years: Grace Matteson, Helen McWorter Simpson, Virgil Burdick, and most of all Juliet Walker.

Grace Matteson (1901–1978) worked as a journalist for the *Pike County Republican* and served as president of the Pike County Historical Society. Born Grace Fish in Baylis, a village five miles northeast of New Philadelphia, she probably grew up with McWorters and oth-

Left, Grace Matteson. *Photo courtesy of Kathy Cabana.*
Right, "Free Frank" McWorter and the "Ghost Town" of New Philadelphia, Pike County, Illinois *(1992) by Grace Matteson. Photo courtesy of the McWorter family.*

ers from the town. Her 1964 manuscript was later republished as a booklet by the Pike County Historical Society: *"Free Frank" McWorter and the "Ghost Town" of New Philadelphia, Pike County, Illinois,* and included photos, drawings, and memories from Larry Burdick. In the manuscript, she gives a good example of remembering:

> On Sunday, April 26 of this year [1964—eds.], Mr. and Mrs. Ray Johnson, who live on the former Solomon McWorter farm in Hadley township, on which the colored cemetery is located, took three members of the Pike County Historical Society, and LeMoyne Washington of Barry, grandson of James Washington, whose second wife was Mary E. McWorter, granddaughter of Free Frank, to see if we could locate the graves of the Negroes who are mentioned in the foregoing story.
>
> The road (?) to the cemetery wound around, through a grove, uphill and down, across gullies and over pasture

Helen McWorter Simpson. Photo courtesy of the McWorter family.

land. With violets, Dutchmen's breeches and May apples peeping through the dead leaves and debris which had washed up onto the bank during recent rains, the ride was not at all unpleasant, although a bit rough.

Mr. Johnson drove a tractor, with LeMoyne standing behind him. They had placed a board across the bed of a four-wheel trailer for two of us to ride on; the other two women rode with their feet dangling out the rear end of the bed-sometimes having to hold their feet in the air to avoid dragging them in the mud as we rode through the deep muddy ruts.

We rode right up to the cemetery gate. The cemetery, which was no doubt once a pretty place, with shade trees here and there, is overgrown now with brambles, briars, and covered with an accumulation of dead leaves, so that it was difficult to find the graves....With the men doing the heavy and digging, quite a number of stones were unearthed, one of them being the marker for a woman nearly 106 years old. This was Judy Armstead, born in 1800, who died in 1906. (from pages 31-33)

Helen McWorter Simpson was a great-granddaughter of Frank

This is the first actual book on the New Philadelphia McWorter family, published in 1981. Photo courtesy of the McWorter family.

and Lucy McWorter. She wrote and published a book about her family in 1981. Helen was the first member of the McWorter family to attend the University of Chicago. She started there in 1914 and earned a PhB. degree in 1918, becoming the third African American woman ever to earn a degree there, followed by her daughter, Helen, in 1953. (The PhB. was a four-year undergraduate program that accepted talented high school students after they completed 10th grade.) While living in Cleveland, she did research on her family and self-published a book on her family and her husband's family. In it she tells how she and her daughter reconstructed family memory:

> We went to Pittsfield, Springfield, and Barry, Illinois where we went through family records. With this information in hand, I felt that I could tell a credible story about the McWorters.... I bought a biography of my great grandfather, Frank

McWorter written by Grace Matteson of Pittsfield and Helen bought a History of Pike County, Illinois written by Jess M. Thompson. Helen was not usually too easily impressed but seemed overwhelmed by the high esteem in which her great great grandfather had been held by the people among whom he had lived and worked. (From the introduction and page 113)

Larry Burdick grew up in New Philadelphia. In a 1992 recollection he recounts the story of his origins. His memory focuses on the house build by his father Virgil Burdick:

> I grew up in this house. I was born in 1928 and we lived in this house until we built a new house in 1941. This house was "added on" twice and perhaps three times. What we used for a living room and bed rooms was clearly the oldest. The room we used for a dining room was probably built on later. I believe this because the floor construction was clearly different than the old part. What we used for a kitchen was added by Tom Preston, who was the owner previous to my father. The back porch which was also shelter over the basement door was added by my father who was a carpenter.
>
> The original part of the house sat on limestone rocks for a foundation. In the winter the wind sifted between the rocks chilled the floors enough to make your teeth chatter. The walls were not boxed in. My mother used to say that the only thing between us and the outside was a little bit of weatherboard. (Virgil Burdick 1992, page 49 in Matteson 1964 reprinted later by Pike County Historical Society)

Beyond the written record, the primary conduit of memory was the oral history of family networks. A democratic message traveled across six or more generations about a remarkable enslaved African American who freed 16 family members, and a diverse frontier community that thrived at a time of great racist strife. Thelma McWorter Kirkpatrick Wheaton (1907-2001) spread this message across many states for many decades. Like Helen, she was a great-granddaughter of Free Frank and Lucy. Thelma carried the tradition of her grand-

Left, A portrait of Thelma McWorter at age 26.
Right, Thelma McWorter later in life.
Photos courtesy of the McWorter family.

mother who raised her, for Thelma's mother died young. As a result, Thelma was closer to the 19th century and the early stories of New Philadelphia than many of her peers. Yet as a young woman she left New Philadelphia also, eventually becoming a community leader in 20th-century Chicago.

A detailed reminiscence by Thelma recently came to light. In it she remembers high school life in Barry:

> During my Freshman year, I lived with my "Auntie" Thomas and Cousin Carrie on Tremont Street [in Barry]. Most Sunday evenings or very early Monday mornings, my father would drive to Barry in a buggy with one horse. When the weather was so cold and freezing my Grandmother insisted on us having heated bricks for our feet so they would not get frostbite. If the weather was too bad, storming or snowing, I would get to take the train from the Hadley station to Barry.

> Family Reunions
> Thelma H. Wheaton
>
> Our individual McWorter families, those by blood and those by marriage, have survived because our cohesiveness, support and resilience with each of the seven generations that we know about from 1771 till now, in spite of the migratory patterns through the years of slavery and of course more modern times.
>
> Through the years our families have made new and modern changes keeping abreast of the times in spite of the social forces that could affect family life. In our families we have tried to develop a healthy self concept, dignity, confidence and unity from early childhood throughout life. We have emphasized that family members need each other no matter what age. In fact intergenerational ideals are growing and developing. Caring, sharing and loving have been and are considered essential for survival and was taught through example by Free Frank and Free Lucy McWorter, their children, one specifically Solomon McWorter, my grandfather and grandmother Frances Jane Coleman McWorter, my father Arthur McWorter and mother Ophelia Walker McWorter, my two sisters, my two brothers, myself and now all the present, 5th, 6th and 7th young generations.
>
> The first First Family Reunion I remember was in 1914 the year my Mother died. There were others before that as told by both my paternal and maternal Grandmothers, Aunts, Uncles and Cousins. These Family Reunions have been a support and network of great strength and stability. They have provided the intergenerational support, the value of which is most difficult to estimate and could

Thelma McWorter, "Family Reunions, pt. 1." Photo courtesy of the McWorter family.

> Some of my classmates who lived in Barry were Lois Strubinger, Alice Hendricks, Glenna Hankins, Corine Jones the Baptist minister's daughter, Ada Hope Nations, Ethel Robb, Frances Sykes, Clarence Coffman, Howard Krieder, and

> of a greater unity. Those who have excelled or achieved fame will be recognized and if at all possible rewarded with a certificate or gift. Those of mature years will be shown the appreciation, the esteem and gratitude for their understanding and support of their respective families and of course a grateful thanks for all the information received that will add to the genealogical history of the family.
>
> (If time permits) I will show and tell about several of our Family Reunions)

Thelma McWorter, "Family Reunions, pt. 2." Part of the document is lost. Photo courtesy of the McWorter family.

> LaVeda Whittekind. Some of the other classmates were Margaret Hackard, Mildred Graybal, Thelma Askew, Geneva Nichols, Nellie Sims, Ruth Sims, Frances Davis, Paul Bennet, William Gray, Lois Pryor, Edna Lee, Chester Welton, Annis Childress, Erma Gamble, Jean Lippencott, Edith Campbell, and Arthur Lippencott the tallest in the class.
>
> Another year I lived school days with Mrs. Bela (Mary Jane Metcalf) Wright. She was the grandmother of Jennie Gleckler.... It was always a pleasure walking rapidly downhill, and on through the town crossing Main Street in the early morning when my energy was at its highest trying never to be late. (Barry Historical Museum 2016, page 15)

After graduating from Barry High School in 1924, Thelma McWorter enrolled at Fisk University in Nashville, Tennessee, earning her degree in 1929. Fisk was a leading center of Black intellectual history, but while she was there it had white leadership and was under the influence of mainstream thinking. One of her professors, the famous Black sociologist Charles Johnson, said in class that most Black families did not know their history. To demonstrate that McWorter family history was not only known, but documented and a living part of their memory, she gathered up family documents on her next trip home and shared them with him and others at Fisk. This was fortunate, because a fire destroyed the family home and the historical materials she had not brought were lost. According to what we know so far, hers have since been the largest collection of materials saved from New Philadelphia.

In "Family Reunions," Thelma McWorter defines family in terms of formal and informal relations. She writes in part:

> Our individual McWorter families, those by blood and those by marriage have survived because our cohesiveness, support and resilience with each of the seven generations that we know about from 1771 till now, in spite of the migratory patterns through the years of slavery and of course more modern times. Through the years our families have made new and modern changes keeping abreast of the times in spite of the social forces that could affect family life. In our families we have tried to develop a healthy self concept, dignity, self-confidence and unity from early childhood throughout life. We have emphasized that family members need each other no matter what age. In fact intergenerational ideals are growing and developing. Caring, sharing and loving have been and are considered essential for survival and was taught through example by Free Frank and Free Lucy McWorter, their children, specifically one son Solomon McWorter my grandfather and grandmother Frances Jane Coleman McWorter, my father Arthur McWorter and mother Ophelia Walker McWorter, my two sisters, my two brothers, myself and now all the present 5th, 6th, and 7th young generations. The first Family Reunion I remember was in 1914 the year my Mother died. There were other reunions before that as told by both my paternal and maternal Grandmothers, Aunts, Uncles and Cousins. These Family Reunions have been a support and network of great strength and stability. They

Thelma Wheaton remembered New Philadelphia in her painting. Photo by Jaclyn Nash.

have provided the intergenerational support, the value of which is most difficult to estimate and could [speak] of a greater unity. Those who have excelled or achieved fame will be recognized and if at all possible rewarded with a certificate or gift. Those of mature years will be shown the appreciation, the esteem and gratitude for their understanding and support of their respective families and of course a grateful thanks for all the information received that will add to the genealogical history of the Family. (If time permits I will show and tell about several of our Family Reunions.)

Thelma McWorter taught elementary school for 50 years and was a national activist and genealogist who kept McWorter descendants linked and aware of their family history. She maintained relationships with people in Pike County through correspondence and annual visits, and she played an active role in the Black memory

Left, Cover, Journal of the Illinois Historical Society, *Emancipation Centennial issue, autumn 1963.*
Right, *Discussion of Frank McWorter and New Philadelphia in an article by Sylvestre C. Watkins, Sr. in the same journal issue. Photos courtesy of the McWorter family.*

institutions in Chicago, Illinois.

Thelma was a great correspondent. She used, created, and kept both documents and photos. She also kept in touch—through letters, cards, reunions, and the Greyhound bus—with a wide network of people: family and friends, Black and white. In this way she kept the memory of New Philadelphia alive and fresh. She painted two landscapes of New Philadelphia, one shown here and the other in chapter four. Details from the two paintings have been authenticated by other sources. When Thelma joined Dr. Margaret Burroughs in founding the DuSable Museum of African American History in

Left, Painting of Free Frank McWorter by Anna McCollough.
Right, Cover, Illinois Negro Historymakers. *Images courtesy of the McWorter family.*

Chicago, materials about the McWorter family and New Philadelphia were part of the museum's opening exhibit in 1961. They remain in the collection today and that museum has just become an affiliate of the Smithsonian Institution.

In 1963 both Thelma and Dr. Burroughs were involved in celebrating the centennial of the 1863 Emancipation Proclamation. Dr. Burroughs commissioned Anna McCollough to paint a portrait of "Free Frank" McWorter to be part of an exhibit hosted by the American Negro Emancipation Centennial Authority. And so the painting hung at McCormick Place in Chicago in 1963, in an exhibit called "A Century of Negro Progress." A photo of the painting was also published in a volume called *Illinois Negro Historymakers*. Today the painting hangs in the DuSable Museum.

In the 1970s Thelma's oldest daughter, Juliet Walker, began the first-ever scholarly research on New Philadelphia. This became her doctoral dissertation, completed at the University of Chicago under the direction of Dr. John Hope Franklin. In part because of her mother, Juliet's early life had been surrounded by reflections on Black history: in the DuSable Museum, the South Side Communi-

Right, Carter G. Woodson. Photo from Scurlock Studio Records, Archives Center, National Museum of American History, Smithsonian Institution. **Left,** Juliet Walker and her two sons, James and Jeffrey. Photo courtesy of the McWorter family.

ty Art Center, at home, and through church activities and family gatherings. The story of her ancestors became the subject of her 1976 doctoral dissertation. In 1983 the University of Kentucky Press published Juliet's first book as *Free Frank: A Black Pioneer on the Antebellum Frontier.* The detailed book was later reprinted.

Juliet's advisor John Hope Franklin was the leading Black historian of his generation and had been educated in the tradition of Carter G. Woodson. Woodson earned an undergraduate degree from the University of Chicago in 1908 and a PhD from Harvard in 1912. He became was the greatest proponent of Black history in the 20th century. In 1926 he created the Association for the Study of Negro Life and History, now the Association for the Study of Afro-American Life and History. Thelma McWorter joined in the organization in the 1930s and promoted the memory of New Philadelphia in the Chicago chapter that hosted its founding convention. Since her graduate school research Juliet has been an active participant in the annual meeting, often speaking on some aspect of Frank McWorter and his work in New Philadelphia. Her focus has especially been on his role as an entrepreneur. She is also the founding director of the Free Frank New Philadelphia Historic Preservation Foundation.

NEGRO HISTORYMAKERS

Some used the Illinois River, which slashed across the state diagonally. Other routes wound from farm to farm, from town to town. During the existence of the Underground Railroad it is estimated that nearly 6,000 slaves escaped the bondage of the slave states and achieved freedom in the north. Only a minor fraction of this total remained in the state of Illinois.

One man who was not dependent on the Underground Railroad was Frank McWorter. He was born a slave in South Carolina in 1777 and was sold to a Kentucky planter at the age of eighteen. After working as a slave for several years, Frank hired his own time, and substituted an annual cash payment for his slave labor. He then began to manufacture saltpetre and by the time he was forty, he had saved enough money so that he was able to pay his owner an agreed sum in return for his freedom.

Frank remained in Kentucky until he had purchased the freedom of his wife Lucy. Then the couple and their three free-born children moved to Illinois—thirteen children had been born slaves and remained in bondage in Kentucky. They arrived in Hadley Township, Pike County, in 1829.

Frank and his family were the township's first settlers and only residents for two years. As a slave Frank did not have a surname, but he was named McWorter by a special act of the Illinois legislature in 1837. Frank built up a successful farm and stock-raising business, and with the money it brought in, he bought freedom for all of his children and two of his grandchildren in Kentucky. In his lifetime, McWorter spent about $10,000 purchasing freedom for himself and his family. When he died in 1854, his will provided funds to free his remaining four grandchildren.

Half a Century of the "Underground"

The Underground Railroad existed, and was operative in most states north of the slaveholding ones for nearly half a century. Many Negroes chose to go to Canada following the Revolutionary War and the War of 1812 because they could achieve emancipation there. After the War of 1812 more and more free Negroes chose to leave their new homes in Canada, journey south to the border states, and then lead families, relatives, and friends, through the "underground" routes they themselves had once taken.

By 1815, many of these routes had been more or less permanently established. They continued for another half century. The end of

15

Juliet Walker's dissertation, published in 1983 by the University of Kentucky Press. Image courtesy of the McWorter family.

Various New Philadelphia families left Pike County for other places in Illinois or beyond, but kept in touch with friends and relatives by mail. Stories of visits and contacts became part of family oral history. Families who remember their contact with McWorters in the 1940s and 1950s include the Johnsons, the Glecklers, and the Burdicks, among others. In 1946 a four-year-old Gerald McWorter visited the Ray Johnson farm (photo, page 152). This farm was at one time the Solomon McWorter farm, and Gerald's father Festus was friends with the Johnsons. Longtime NPA leader Harry Wright recalls that he was in that field the same day, at work making hay.

According to Harry, his grandfather was providing hay baling services using what the family called the "set still baler"—as opposed to a baler that travels down the field. Harry identified the horse as Barney. On the other side of the haystack, he recalled, was the horse Babe, driven by Howard Harshman. In addition, Harry remembers stories of his Irick great-grandparents near New Philadelphia. In 2016 he told how his great-great-grandfather came to the area and borrowed a horse, an ax, and a saw from "Free Frank" McWorter. He aimed to use these to build a cabin on his recently acquired land. Along the way he shared his abolitionist sentiments with Frank McWorter. The next day Frank sent his son Solomon and another man over to help build the cabin.

Harry also mentioned a series of caves in the area that were used by the Underground Railroad in the general area of New Philadelphia. Harry tells how Lucy McWorter was a cobbler and made shoes for people running for their lives through New Philadelphia. Her son Solomon was a cabinetmaker who took his goods for sale to the nearby market towns of Quincy and Jacksonville. During these trips he took African Americans along as helpers who then simply disappeared into the Underground Railroad going North.

The records of the McWorter family and New Philadelphia were mentioned frequently in key state publications when Black history of the state was being featured. Professionals in the memory institutions made these mentions possible, always helping the history stay alive.

Even as people continued to remember New Philadelphia the

Gerald McWorter, age 4, visiting the Ray Johnson farm in or near New Philadelphia. Photo courtesy of the McWorter family.

physical place was emptying out. But that was about to change. Several local people put up a large sign that told the story. Juliet Walker dedicated herself to commemorating the place and with her mother Thelma won federal recognition for one of New Philadelphia's

Article on Juliet Walker's walk from Pulaski County, Kentucky to Barry, Illinois. From The Courier-Journal, *October 3, 1990; Image courtesy of the McWorter family.*

two cemeteries. In 1988 the National Park Service of the United States Department of the Interior announced the inclusion of the Free Frank McWorter Gravesite in the National Register of Historic Places. This was the third grave so honored in Illinois, after those of Abraham Lincoln and Stephen Douglas.

Juliet Walker did not carry out her work as an academic project only, but as a personal and family mission; just one example of her own determination was her 500-mile walk in September-October 1990 from Pulaski County, Kentucky to Barry, Illinois. She followed the same path family documents indicated that Frank and Lucy McWorter took in 1830–31. Her walk drew attention to the town and her ancestor's heroic deeds, and she arrived at her destination in time for the ceremony placing the marker and the subsequent celebration. Her emphasis on place contributed mightily to New Philadelphia's rebirth.

As another way to honor and remember Frank McWorter, Thel-

The program for the event marking the Free Frank Gravesite National Register of Historic Places, October 6, 1990. Image courtesy of the McWorter family.

ma McWorter asked her cousin Shirley McWorter Moss, an engineer just then emerging as a sculptor, to create a bust of Frank. It was her first commission, and is depicted and described more fully at the start of chapter 2. She and her brother William McWorter unveiled the sculpture at the DuSable Museum of African American History in Chicago. Another cast of the bust is at the Abraham Lincoln Presidential Library & Museum in Springfield.

As we will see in the next chapter, landowner and farmer Larry

Presentation of bust of Frank McWorter to Abraham Lincoln Presidential Library. **Left to right,** *Sandra McWorter, Delores Kirkpatrick, Allen Kirkpatrick, Darlene Kirkpatrick, Patricia McWorter, Stewart Moss, Shirley McWorter Moss, and Mary and Ron Carter.*

Armistead moved several old log cabins onto the empty foundations of several New Philadelphia buildings. And most important of all, a highway was sought and won, and when it threatened the town, local people (led by the chair of the highway commission) organized themselves into the New Philadelphia Association to see that the site had survived as a place. Not quite ten years later, they had recruited historians and archaeologists. These scholars found funding to study New Philadelphia, including from the federal National Science Foundation. Seven years of research brought waves of students as research assistants. A few of the students were even descendants of New Philadelphia families. All this activity enthused and educated more people. It brought descendant families back to the area.

They visited. They held a reunion. They visited again. They joined the New Philadelphia Association and invested in New Philadelphia. And so the next chapter turns to the rebirth of New Philadelphia.

Chapter Six

Rebirth

In the best of cases, remembering involves three things. First, our mental capacity to retain thoughts and feelings about the past. Second, artifacts and documents from the past. Finally, our individual and collective imagining. Social institutions such as museums and monuments anchor this imagining. But a remembered place can become once again a place of human activity aimed at unearthing, recreating, and retelling that past. That is when memory becomes rebirth.

Rebirth of the past creates new experiences for reliving the past. This is the new mission of memory institutions, to awaken the past and help new generations interact with artifacts and documents. Memory specialists use both science and art to unearth, retell, and recreate past experience.

So far seven parties have taken the lead in bringing about New Philadelphia's rebirth. Larry and Natalie Armistead owned the land that was New Philadelphia. Local leaders organized as the New Philadelphia Association invested their time and money and recruited others. Descendants of Frank and Lucy McWorter returned to the area individually and in groups, including historian Juliet E. K. Walker. The University of Illinois at Springfield and the Illinois State Museum activated professionals and funds towards preserving and studying local state heritage. A team of archaeologists from several research universities carried out scientific research and teaching at New Philadelphia. And the federal government provided both recognition and funding. Each of these had different motivations, but they have been able to converge and collaborate for close to 20 years,

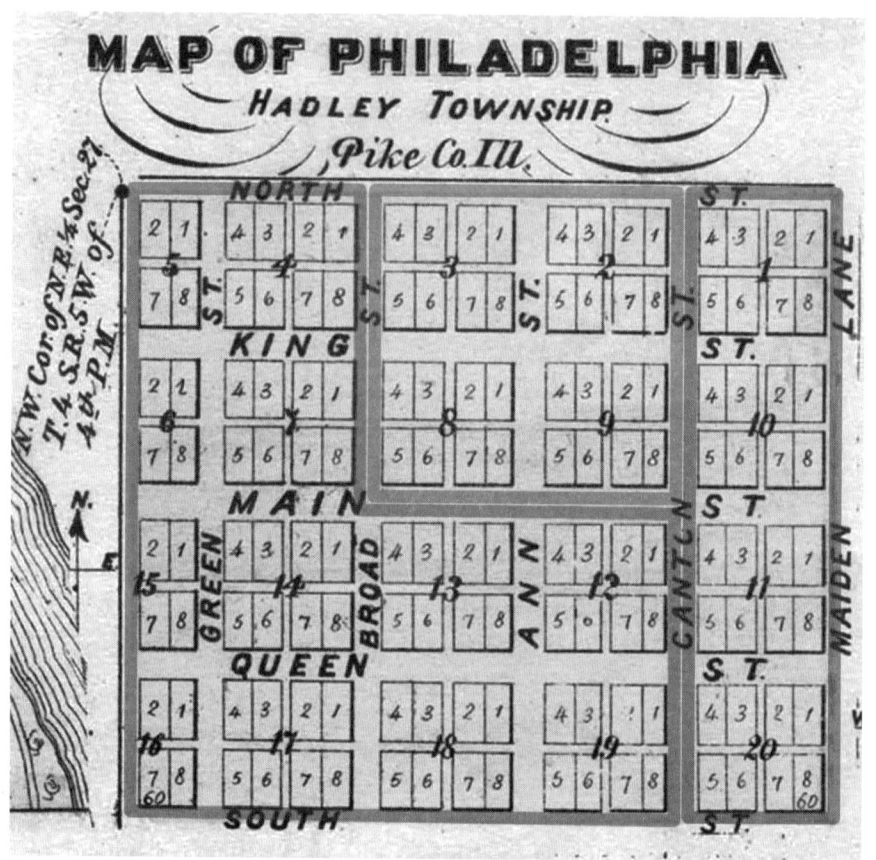

This early printed map of New Philadelphia is still useful today. As of February 2018, blocks 1, 10, 11, 20 are owned by the Philadelphia Land Trust, Larry Armistead, trustee. Blocks 3, 2, 8, 9 are owned by the Archaeological Conservancy. The other blocks are owned by the New Philadelphia Association. From Ensign 1872, page 84. Public domain.

1998 through to today.

Over the years the New Philadelphia Association acquired land from Larry Armistead's Philadelphia Land Trust, the Burdick family, and the Arnett family. NPA bought the land shown here as well as a lane to the nearby cemetery and land immediately around the cemetery. The cemetery is owned by the county.

The Armisteads, the Burdicks, and the Arnetts all wanted to

Left, Natalie Ballenger Armistead, Larry Armistead's wife, who was an advocate and activist for remembering New Philadelphia and served as vice president of the New Philadelphia Association.
Middle, Wayne Riley and Carol McCartney at the New Philadelphia sign. Photo courtesy of Phil Bradshaw.
Right, Judge Cecil J. Burrows. Photo courtesy of the Pike County Courthouse Victim Witness Coordinator's Office.

help preserve the place for remembering New Philadelphia. Because the archaeological work—informally referred to as the dig—was so significant and visible among researchers, the Archaeological Conservancy in turn bought some of the land from the New Philadelphia Association. As the New Philadelphia Association raises funds and pays off the mortgage on its land, ownership continues to stabilize and safeguard New Philadelphia for the future. This chapter tells the story of how this and so much more came to be.

A comment made in 1999 by Natalie Armistead expressed the sentiments of people in Pike County. It was captured in the minutes of a New Philadelphia Association meeting: "She doesn't want things in a glass case. She wants something that people can touch and learn." Her husband Larry has always agreed with this, arguing for an annual event for recreation and retelling that can sustain rebirth. Descendant and historian Juliet Walker has always envisioned building a partial replica of the actual town of New Philadelphia.

Those who remembered the stories of New Philadelphia always cared about the place. The farmers who owned the land remembered and cared. In 1964, Grace Matteson and other local history buffs rode on the back of a tractor through field and stream to see the New Philadelphia cemetery for themselves. A 1977 newspaper account mentions a four-foot-wide sign marking the town site. These were short-lived interventions, and there was more to come.

For by the 1990s, local farmers and leaders were ready to attend to the place that was New Philadelphia. The Central Illinois Expressway, later identified as Interstate 72, was well under construction, passing not even 100 feet from the cemetery. The interstate opened to traffic in November 1991. The negotiations for public highway construction funds and for right-of-ways with every farmer and landowner along the path had been prolonged and painstaking. One of the farmer-landowners in negotiation with the committee was Larry Armistead. In the end, the highway passed close to the New Philadelphia town site and cemetery without incorporating access to the cemetery as McWorter descendants had urged. The construction impacted the flow of Kiser Creek, which ran between the cemetery and New Philadelphia. The interstate separated the former town from its graves in a second cemetery known by then as the Johnson cemetery. Along its path, the highway cut around or through farms. Towns lobbied for highway exits, with or without success. All of this unfolded with a view towards ending the area's isolation and facilitating economic development.

And yet, the committee that negotiated the path of the highway through Pike and adjacent counties was very much aware of and concerned with New Philadelphia. As its work concluded, committee chair Phil Bradshaw and others took up the issue of preserving and if possible developing the site.

By 1996 a group of volunteers had united to erect a new sign at New Philadelphia. They embedded it in a stone-and-concrete base. In 1998 they organized as the New Philadelphia Association. The incorporation papers identify Cecil J. Burrows as agent; at that point he was in his 28th year (photo, page 159 top, right) as Illinois' 8th Circuit Judge. The first meeting minutes and legal documents identify people who initiated and maintained the local history work that resulted in the rebirth of New Philadelphia. There were Griggsville pig farmer and highway commission chair Philip Bradshaw, who has served as the association's chairperson, and his wife Linda. Bradshaws have been in Pike County for over a century, having arrived in the 1890s. Phil chaired the highway advocacy group AMPS (named for Adams, Morgan, Pike, and Scott Counties), and his son Todd learned about New Philadelphia at college from his professor, Juliet Walker. As the highway was built, Phil made a commitment to see New Philadelphia protected and, as it happened, reborn. Phil has also been active for decades in national and international pork and soybean marketing.

There too were Natalie Ballenger Havey (later Armistead) and Larry Armistead, who owned and farmed most of the New Philadelphia land. Carol McCartney was on hand, bringing her knowledge and skills from engagement in several local history groups as well as the writing of history, in particular that of New Philadelphia, as part of her column in and taking photographs for the *Pike County Express*. She has been Secretary of the New Philadelphia Association since August 2002, taking over from founding secretary Shirley Johnston. Farmer Wayne Riley was there as well, a pork griller extraordinaire who developed his own Riley's Seasonings, which grew into a family business in 1974. Tom Coulson, editor and publisher of the *Pike County Express,* was also there from the start.

Harry Wright was there from the beginning. For decades he was the University of Illinois extension agent for Pike County. Harry traces his family back to Pike County when New Philadelphia was founded. His wife and local librarian Helen Wright volunteered with him. Harry Wright is a descendant of farmers who helped and were helped by McWorters and other New Philadelphians. He first learned about segregation as an 11 year old while working with his uncle and LeMoyne Washington, an African American descendant of New Philadelphia and longtime farm worker in Northern Pike County. Harry served for many decades on the County Board and the NPA; his wife Helen, a retired librarian, served as NPA's treasurer. Harry wrote in a 2005 NPA newsletter:

Left, Linda Bradshaw. Photo courtesy of Pittsfield Rotary Club.
Right, Phil Bradshaw. Photo courtesy of Abraham Lincoln Presidential Library & Museum.

I saw part of New Philadelphia in the late 1930s when I stayed with my grandparents and Uncle Jake Iftner, all of whom were close friends of LeMoyne Washington. Several McWorters who lived away from here were also visitors in my Uncle's home in Hadley Township in the 50s and 60s. After a long visit with LeMoyne, I wrote a newspaper story about New Philadelphia in the late 80s. I became hooked when the Rotary Club proposed the installation of a new sign there. I helped Phil Bradshaw in getting the project started. It is something that needs to be done to preserve the history of the region, the town, and to establish Free Frank McWorter's place in history.

LeMoyne Washington and I had a 60+ year friendship and I treasure the memories and lessons I learned from him. He was the first black man I ever saw. I am proud to be a part of NPA, and I really appreciate meeting the many members of the McWorter family.

May we proceed in reaching for recognition and preservation of New Philadelphia so that this will be a place visited by those interested in the real history of our country and its people.

Left, Carol McCartney. Photo courtesy of Andrea King.
Middle, Harry Wright. Photo courtesy of Pittsfield Rotary Club.
Right, Helen Wright. Photo courtesy of Andrea King.

Another Interstate 72 activist was also on hand: Joe Conover, the retired editor of the *Quincy Herald-Whig*, with his wife Jane. He ended up serving as vice-chair of the New Philadelphia Association for two decades until 2014. In addition, he served on the Quincy Highway Committee and was a former director of the Dr. Richard Eells House, which commemorates the Quincy doctor who helped Charley and others escape to freedom after crossing the Mississippi River. The United States Supreme Court reviewed the case of Dr. Eells and the freedom seeker Charley, described in Chapter 1, and this served to mobilize public opinion against slavery.

Other participants included J. Terry Ransom, the state's most prominent Illinois Underground Railroad researcher, who published a map of the known routes to freedom across the state; longtime civic leader from the county seat of Pittsfield, Shirley Johnston; and Shari Marshall, superintendent of the Barry school system. Two more New Philadelphia descendants who have served on the board are Chicagoan Sandra McWorter Marsh, Frank and Lucy's great-great-granddaughter, and Ron Carter, who wrote in that same 2005 NPA newsletter, "I live in Springfield, Illinois. Because my aunt Irene Butler Brown and her parents, William and Katie Butler, lived in New Philadelphia, I have met some of the most dedicated, nicest

Left, Lonie Wilson, sixth-generation descendant of "Free Frank" McWorter. After connecting her wing of the family with the 2005 McWorter family reunion, she alerted descendants in Texas and Colorado and joined the board of the NPA. Photo by Kate Williams-McWorter.
Right, Joe Conover. Photo courtesy of Joe Conover.

people in the world. I speak of the members of the NPA."

Pat Likes, former English professor at nearby Hannibal-LaGrange College, local history advocate, and writer and photographer (again for the *Pike County Express*) joined early on. She went on to be a long-time member of the New Philadelphia Association board and one of its main photographers. Here is how she begins one of her tellings of the New Philadelphia story:

> The story of New Philadelphia, in Hadley Township, Pike County, Illinois, is a love story.
> It is the story of love between a man and a woman, love between that couple and their family, love between that family and the freedom that enabled them to create a community on the Illinois frontier. (Likes, no date, page 1)

With Pat came her husband Marvin Likes, a leading land surveyor in the region. The original plat commissioned by Frank McWorter in the 1830s proved to be an exact match to Marvin's first survey for the New Philadelphia Association in the 1990s. Marvin's

This group portrait captures most of those who attended the 2005 McWorter family reunion. Photo by Ginny Lee, used with permission.

team, sometimes including his late son Tom, carried out many surveys for the archaeologists and others working on New Philadelphia, always at no cost. The NPA organizes the Marvin and Thomas Likes Lecture Series every June. It was named in their honor and focuses on history and the freedom struggle.

The purpose of the NPA was set out as:

> The commemoration, preservation, exposition, research, and teaching of Pike County, Illinois history in general and specifically that of the settlement of New Philadelphia, platted in 1836, and that of its creator, "Free Frank" McWorter, a former slave.

More recently the New Philadelphia Association has welcomed Lonie Wilson, Douglas King, Brenda Middendorf, Kaye and David Iftner, and Marynel and Jerry Corton onto its board and McWorter descendant Sheena Franklin as consultant. Doug founded the Springfield and Central Illinois African American History Museum. Brenda Middendorf is Executive Director of Two Rivers Resource Conservation and Development Area. Kaye is executive director of the Pike County Chamber of Commerce. David and Marynel trace their families as local back to the early to mid-1800s, David to the

Marvin and Pat Likes. Photo courtesy of Pat Likes.

Irick family and Marynel in two ways. She is descended from William Freeman who in 1833, with Frank McWorter and Brother Martin, represented the Barry Baptist Church at a church meeting near Blue River. And she is also descended from the Hull family of Hadley Township, who helped pay the mortgage that built the 1854 brick Baptist Church in Barry. She and her husband worship there today.

Natalie and Larry Armistead had already found New Philadelphia artifacts as they walked and worked their land. The group decided to work towards archaeology and restoration of the cemetery, researching the physical town site, and eventually creating a visitor's center. Marvin Likes donated his time for surveying. Pat reached out to Juliet Walker. Members brainstormed about recruiting African Americans to the project. A Barry High School class, including Larry Armistead's daughter Shaylin Armistead, studied New Philadelphia.

Hearing about the effort, local farmer Roy Stickhorst let the new association know that he had 18th-century New Philadelphia documents that his parents had found in their house. Could the New Philadelphia Association help him pass those to Professor Walker? This all happened in just the first year of the NPA's all-volunteer effort.

Left, While there are no remaining structures from the original town of New Philadelphia, Larry Armistead led the way in relocating three structures from that period from other sites in Pike County. Photo courtesy of Joe Conover.
Right, This 1998 photo by Loretta Ann Owings shows Larry Armistead, John Mangham, and Wayne Lawber reassembling one of the cabins. Used with permission of the photographer.

During the second year of the NPA, Larry Armistead had obtained a 19th-century log cabin from his brother-in-law Roger Sleeper and rebuilt it on the site. A second cabin came from Tommy Hughes. It was soon named the blacksmith shop, based on its size, the tools found nearby, the historical record, and oral history. Larry traded Tommy Wombles a 1969 Plymouth Road Runner for a third cabin soon after. These cabins were as old as the first stories of New Philadelphia, and from within Pike County. As Larry and his wife Natalie envisioned, the cabins help visitors identify and imagine the New Philadelphia of the 1800s, and respect what was accomplished there. This vision was shared by many, including the crew in the photo here.

Larry Armistead has owned and farmed the land that includes the former town of New Philadelphia for several decades. As he and Natalie worked the land, they found and collected many farm implements from the time the land was still a thriving town as well as earlier stone tools. Larry took the initiative in many ways to help tell the story of the town. For the cabins, Larry put the word out that he was interested in any old structures that might be available in the region. As the three came his way, he engineered moving them to New Philadelphia and setting them up on 19th-century foundations that were visible in the ground. Help came then and since from Raymond Anderson, Robert Armistead, Kelly and Eric Craigmiles, David Lee, Donald Sapps, Steve Shaw, and Martin Stauffer. Today Larry, Liz Shealor, and Brian Robbins—who once extracted a raccoon from chimney of the Burdick house—are the first-line caretakers of the town site.

Other NPA members focused on recruiting partners to help. Soon Professor Vibert White from the University of Illinois at Springfield (UIS) joined the NPA. Together the NPA and the university reached out to the Illinois State Museum and to Paul Shackel, an archaeologist with the University of Maryland, as well as to leaders in Pike County, McWorter descendants, and the University of Illinois. Vibert led in getting a $50,000 grant from his university to help start New Philadelphia's rebirth. On a volunteer basis with expenses covered by UIS and the NPA itself, amateurs, professionals, and students began the history and archaeology that formed the basis for New Philadelphia's rebirth.

Through the grapevine, spurred by attentive local media, Pike Countians and descendants of New Philadelphia mobilized. Larry and Natalie Armistead found more buildings dating from the founding of the town and rebuilt them in New Philadelphia. The New Philadelphia Association acquired the sole remaining 20th-century home in the town. It was the Virgil Burdick farmhouse from 1941, with outbuildings, shown in chapter 4. The Burdicks had farmed in New Philadelphia since the mid-1800s.

A walkover of the town site took place, with dozens of people carefully stepping and planting flags where they spotted artifacts. Before they could begin the land was plowed. Doing the plowing was Roger Wood, the owner of land once part of Frank McWorter's farm across from the town. The walkover found a total of 7,073 items. Roughly 5,932 of the artifacts were from the European and African American settlement period. The remaining 1,141 were from earlier Native American settlement. Using high-tech methods, the archae-

Left, University of Central Florida Professor Vibert White, formerly at the University of Illinois at Springfield. Photo from the Orlando Sentinel. *Right*, In 2002, the Researching and Preserving African-American Frontier Settlements conference was organized by Vibert White at the University of Illinois at Springfield. The event brought together descendants, local advocates, and scholars to focus on New Philadelphia's rebirth.

ologists then looked beneath the surface without disturbing the soil. The results pointed to where even more artifacts might be found. With these first finds as well as the strong combination of local activists and well-connected professionals, funding from the National Science Foundation became a possibility. Paul Shackel took the lead on grantwriting. NSF eventually provided two grants that spanned

2004-2011 for an archaeological project at New Philadelphia. The University of Illinois at Urbana Champaign funded years of work as well. All along, the project was also a professional training program for graduate and undergraduate students.

The archaeology work was a collaboration of faculty, staff, and students at the Illinois State Museum, the University of Illinois at Urbana Champaign and at Springfield, the University of Maryland at College Park, the Construction Engineering Research Laboratory (U. S. Army Corps of Engineers) and the New Philadelphia Association. A great deal of formal planning and research design goes into what people informally call a dig; ultimately 17 New Philadelphia town lots were excavated from 2004 to 2011. Paul Shackel, Christopher Fennell, Anna Agbe-Davies, Terry Martin, Claire Martin, Michael Hargrave, Michelle Huttes, and Charlotte King were key to this effort. Paul was one of the main scholars who led the National Science Foundation-sponsored field school at New Philadelphia. Not only did he train students and always collaborate with the NPA, he also wrote several scholarly works on the New Philadelphia project (see bibliography). Christopher Fennell is an archaeologist at the University of Illinois at Urbana Champaign. A research partner of Paul Shackel's, Chris also won University of Illinois funding for several summers of archaeology field schools at New Philadelphia. He maintains a website that contains most of the research data and documentation from the dig, as well as library and government document research. Anna, an archaeologist at the University of North Carolina, joined the New Philadelphia dig when on the faculty of DePaul University in Chicago. Her historical expertise includes some of the household objects that were unearthed in the dig.

Terry Martin, for many years Curator and Chair of Anthropology at the Illinois State Museum, has been one of the four main professional archaeologists on the New Philadelphia dig, active now for close to 20 years. He directed the archiving of more than 150,000 artifacts, plant remains, and animal remains that were discovered at the site during 2002-2011 and has presented on New Philadelphia at many scholarly professional meetings.

Surveying the site to guide the archaeology. Digging for artifacts began with precise measurements of the geographical location of New Philadelphia. Photo courtesy of Claire Martin.

These items are now owned by the State of Illinois and housed at the Illinois State Museum unless they are on loan for exhibit at other institutions. Claire Martin, also affiliated with the Illinois State Museum, is the professional historian who has been active alongside the archaeologists. She has focused on information in libraries and government archives—county and state documents as well as census information. In addition, she helped collect oral histories from descendants of New Philadelphia.

Michael Hargrave led several seasons of geophysical surveys, working with and training the student teams. These surveys use equipment to measure magnetic and electrical resistance in the soil that point to unusual spots underground that might be good to excavate. Michelle Huttes, then a graduate student in history as well as an employee of Archer Daniels Midland in Decatur, Illinois, took the lead in preparing the documentation for adding New Philadelphia to the National Register of Historic Places in August 2005.

The Pike Press in Pittsfield, Illinois, 14 miles southeast of New Philadelphia, has consistently reported on its rebirth. This cartoon by Bill Beard is just one way that local media communicated what was going on at New Philadelphia. Reproduced with permission of the artist and the Pike Press.

Charlotte King began her contribution with undergraduate thesis work on New Philadelphia and then served as lab director of the archaeology project from 2004–2006 while she earned a master's degree from the University of Maryland. Among her many contributions, Charlotte wrote two reports. In one, she explains how the cemetery showed signs of African American and African burial practices, connecting New Philadelphians culturally to their origins across the Atlantic, before slavery. In the other, she compiled and analyzed data from six official censuses done in the 19th century to determine the population and demographics of New Philadelphia. She also created a student/teacher guide to New Philadelphia. Charlotte continues as an active spokesperson for New Philadelphia on Capitol Hill, lobbying Congress as well as having kept the NPA informed as national recognition of New Philadelphia proceeded.

One of the remarkable aspects of the archaeology work is that as it unfolded, the results and even the data itself were put online

This iron trivet was one of the larger items excavated at New Philadelphia. It speaks to the blacksmithing going on in the town—of practical and artistic value—and the domestic work of sewing, laundering, and ironing clothes. Photo courtesy of the Illinois State Museum.

where anyone can access it freely, at the University of Maryland, the University of Illinois, and in The Digital Archaeological Record, tDAR.

The recovery of the material artifacts has provided thousands of bits — glass, porcelain, bone, stone structures, pieces of metal, and entire intact items, as well as important clues from patterns in the soil preserved over the years. No object is too small to save, whether it can be assembled into something larger or just provide a clue by itself to help reconstruct what life was like in New Philadelphia. These are like dots that have to be connected to rediscover what life was like, what people ate, the structures they lived in, the stuff they used to live, and any connections to regional, national, and international economics, politics, and culture. Connecting the dots has been guid-

Top, left to right, Paul Shackel. Photo courtesy of Laura Ours, University of Maryland. Christopher Fennell. Photo from University of Illinois, photographer L. Brian Stauffer. Claire Martin. Photo from Quincy Herald-Whig. Charlotte King. Photo courtesy of the Illinois State Museum, photographer Gary Andrashko.
Middle, left to right, Terry Martin and a student. Anna Agbe-Davies. Photos courtesy of Joe Conover.
Bottom, University of Maryland graduate student Charlotte King recording artifacts found on the surface of New Philadelphia's McWorter cemetery. Each flag records one item. The archaeologists carefully surveyed the site and located, identified, and mapped the exact location of material objects deposited on the ground surface, while leaving those objects in place. Photo courtesy of Claire Martin.

Top left, Phil Bradshaw, president of the New Philadelphia Association, and Paul Shackel from the University of Maryland talk about dig progress with a student-archaeologist in the foreground. Whenever rain threatened, the team covered the active dig spots with tarps, as in the background. Photo courtesy of the Abraham Lincoln Presidential Library & Museum.

Top right, University of Illinois Professor Chris Fennell explains the archaeology team's methods and interpretations to Malcolm Gay, a columnist for American Archaeology magazine. Photo by Joe Conover, used with permission.

Bottom left, Oral history, government and other records and documents, and geophysical measurement were three sources guiding the archaeologists. In this photo, a wall and several spots where soil indicated a former post were unearthed by using small trowels to remove the soil carefully and precisely. Photo courtesy of Paul A. Shackel.

Bottom right, After any larger objects are either taken out or left in place as appropriate, soil that has been troweled aside is shoveled into buckets and then sifted. Here George Calfas is sifting to find any smaller objects. Photo courtesy of Joe Conover.

Top, Research station tents were set up to provide space for cleaning and cataloging the found objects. This became the physical manifestation that there was a rebirth of New Philadelphia. Photo by Joe Conover, used with permission.

Middle left, Carrie Christman and Dana Blount sifting for artifacts. Students from Illinois and from around the country participated in the dig. They joined community members who had started the work with key scholars in 2002. Photo courtesy of Paul A. Shackel.

Middle right, Kathryn Fay using a toothbrush to clean shards of glass and porcelain pieces. Photo by Joe Conover, used with permission.

Bottom left, Cleaning went on every day as the rebirth of New Philadelphia was carried out piece by piece. Here Kathryn Fay and Shalonda Collins are hard at work. Photo by Joe Conover, used with permission.

Bottom right, All of the found pieces were organized by type and shape. These kinds of findings are the beginning of reconstructing the objects that begin to tell a story about life in New Philadelphia. Photo by Joe Conover, used with permission.

Top left, Occasionally a whole object is found such as these two bottles marked Quincy, Illinois. The Coca-Cola bottle **(left)** was produced in or after 1905. Photo by Joe Conover, used with permission.

Top middle, Student archaeologist Kathrine Hardcastle holding a bottle that the team found at New Philadelphia. It advertises the Chicago liquor distributor Charles Dennehy and Co. The company name dates back to 1893; the liquor came from Kentucky. Photo courtesy of Anna Agbe-Davies.

Top right, New Philadelphia participated in national and international commerce. This is part of a ceramic container for cosmetic powder or rouge. The House of Dorin was founded in the 18th century to serve French aristocracy; this item dates to ca. 1900. Photo courtesy of Claire Martin.

Bottom left, Once the material findings were cleaned and sorted they were placed in plastic bags and labeled. They were then shipped off to the Illinois State Museum for further classification and study. Photo by Joe Conover, used with permission.

Bottom right, These bone fragments found at New Philadelphia have been combined with historical evidence to compare people's diets with where they came from. Photo by Joe Conover, used with permission.

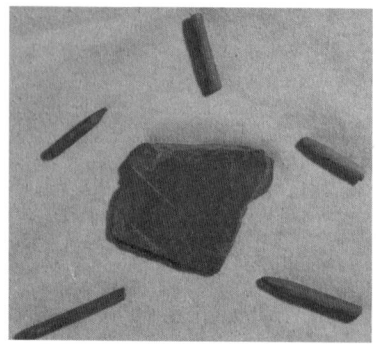 

Left, Pieces of slate used in the school. Photo courtesy of Claire Martin. *Right*, The students engaged in archaeology in New Philadelphia each summer spent July in the Illinois State Museum laboratories in Springfield. They identified and catalogued what had been found each June. Photo by Joe Conover, used with permission.

ed by court records, documents and photographs in various family collections, and oral history. Sometimes the remembered New Philadelphia led to material remains that validated the memory. In other instances the oral history could be neither validated nor denied. The analysis always relied on the imagination of the scholars, local history buffs, and town descendants. At every step of the way there was discussion between the researchers and local residents and history activists.

Just a recent example was in 2016 when Sheri and Chuck Wendorff showed their 19th-century daybook to the New Philadelphia Association. A daybook is a book where a business recorded every transaction before entering it into a ledger book. Wendorff and Company were merchants in Barry for 125 years starting in the 1830s or 40s. Records like these show a much closer view of a locale than a census, which happens only every ten years, property records that exclude people who don't own property, or even old newspapers that don't tell every story. For New Philadelphia, linking information from all these sources with archaeology and other historical sources is still underway.

A second aspect to the rebirth has been virtual: re-creating New

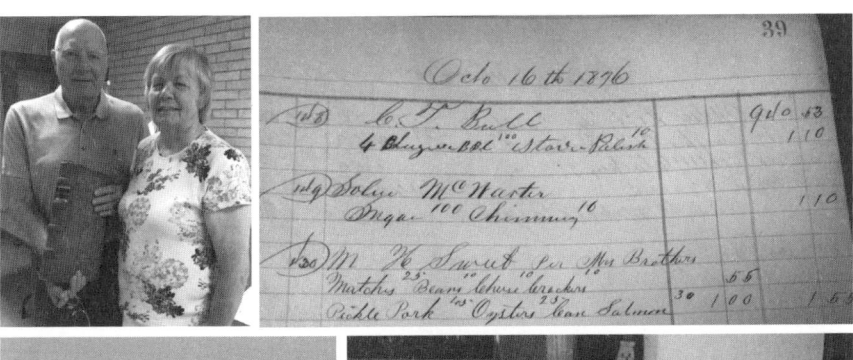

Top left, Sheri and Chuck Wendorff with the daybook that shows transactions with New Philadelphians. Photo by Kate Williams-McWorter.
Top right, One day in October 1876, Solomon McWorter bought sugar for one dollar and a chimney for ten cents. Photo by Kate Williams-McWorter.
Bottom left, Sally and Lettie, a fictional retelling of the New Philadelphia story. Cover image used courtesy of the author.
Bottom right, left to right, grandmother Kathryn (Meyer) Weir, granddaughters Karen Vidlock Petersen and Kathryn Vidlock Granley and mother Rossellyn (Weir) Vidlock. Photo courtesy of K. V. Granley.

Philadelphia online. Besides the augmented reality project underway at the site, there are several websites: the New Philadelphia Association, the University of Illinois, the University of Maryland,

*Designer Jon Amakawa, **in foreground**, shows others a pilot of New Philadelphia in augmented reality. Photo by Kate Williams-McWorter.*

the McWorter family, and the Free Frank New Philadelphia Historic Preservation Foundation, as well as such general websites as Wikipedia. On these sites one can find documents of memory, oral history, and archaeological research data. And the storytelling continues. One fresh example of this is the young people's chapter book *Sally and Lettie* by Kathryn Vidlock Granley (page 179, bottom left and right). The author explains how New Philadelphia stimulated her imagination:

> When I was 10 years old, I was on a car ride from Hull, Illinois, to Pittsfield with my grandmother. She pointed out an area where the Underground Railroad had a station. Many years later I researched and realized it was likely the site of the Frank McWorter home.... For many years, I imagined what it would have been like for slaves to cross into Illinois. I imagined both adults and children and this book is the story that came out of all that imagining. (Vidlock Granley, 2017, no pagination)

Another aspect of the rebirth is being constructed at the local, state, and national level in memory institutions. Museum exhibits frequently aggregate material artifacts to tell a story about the past. The Barry Historical Museum has an exhibit documenting an envisioned reconstruction of New Philadelphia. The story and archaeological artifacts were part of a 2009 exhibit at the Illinois State Museum, "From Humble Beginnings: Lincoln's Illinois 1830-1861." The Lincoln Presidential Library in Springfield, Illinois, has on display the life-size bust of "Free Frank" made by his descendant Shirley McWorter Moss. Kathryn Harris, the library director, provided continuous research support for New Philadelphia, and lectured and performed for the cause, particularly in her one-woman show portraying Harriet Tubman before audiences of all kinds. The Springfield and Central Illinois African American History Museum also featured New Philadelphia and artifacts in a 2017 exhibit titled "Living in Freedom: New Philadelphia and Free Frank McWorter."

The DuSable Museum of African American History in Chicago has the second life-size bust of Free Frank McWorter along with an earlier portrayal of Frank shown in chapter 5. The National Museum of American History has on exhibit items including a bowl and pitcher used by Free Frank's son Solomon McWorter, a child's rocking chair that Solomon made for family members that was used for more than 150 years, images of landscape paintings by Thelma McWorter, and artifacts from the site lent by the Illinois State Museum. This is for their permanent exhibit, "Many Voices, One Nation." The National Museum of African American History and Culture is exhibiting the third life-size bronze bust of Free Frank, and they also have on display the widely adopted textbook *Introduction to Afro-American Studies* written by Gerald McWorter (Abdul Alkalimat), his great-great-grandson.

As of this writing, rebirth continues.

These last few photographs demonstrate the many connections forged in the rebirth of New Philadelphia. To answer Langston Hughes from page one of this book: if we cherish the stories and each other, New Philadelphia can help America be America, the land where every person is free.

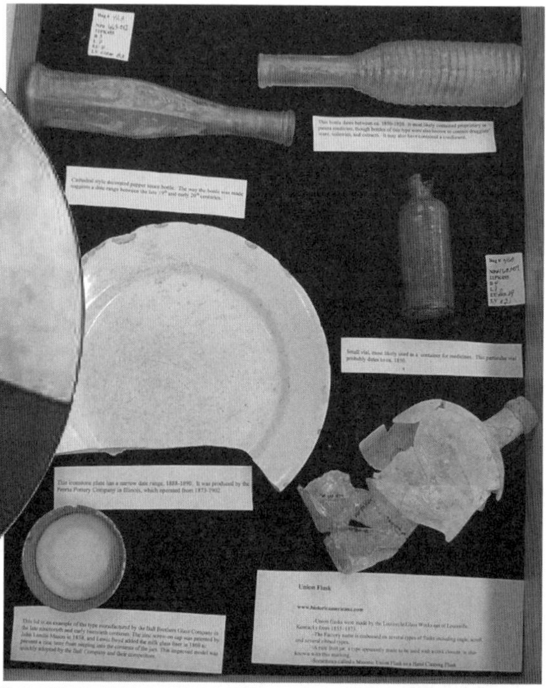

Top left, Kathryn Harris. Photo from Illinois Historic Preservation Agency.
Top right, bottom left, Here are some more of the material remains of New Philadelphia. Some of these artifacts help to recreate how people ate in terms of flatware and utensils.
Bottom right, Among the media that documented the rebirth of New Philadelphia was the Time Team America television program. They produced an episode about the dig which is available at https://www.youtube.com/watch?v=OH88cMRfHYM. Here they are interviewing archaeologist Terry Martin of the Illinois State Museum.

Top left, Many youth groups came to visit and learn from the dig. Putting New Philadelphia in the memory of this young generation is a major aspect of the rebirth of New Philadelphia and what it stood for. Here Anna Agbe-Davies explains the excavation. Photo courtesy of Joe Conover.

Top right, As part of sharing the research of the dig with visitors to New Philadelphia site a wall of information was erected. This contained maps and locations of the material findings of the dig. Here Joe Conover and Wayne Riley examine the information. Photo courtesy of Pat Likes.

Bottom left, A donation is commemorated in this photo of, **left to right,** Dan Arnsman, Instructor Tech at John Wood Community College; Phil Bradshaw; Claire Martin; Sandra McWorter Marsh; and James C. Gay, representing the Illinois Rural Electric Cooperative. The five of them stand in front of the fireplace in the house built in 1941 in New Philadelphia by the Burdick family. Photo courtesy of Claire Martin.

Bottom right, In 2006 the New Philadelphia Association held a Day of Discovery for the descendants of New Philadelphia to gather and share their memories and material from New Philadelphia. Every family shared and learned. Photo courtesy of Claire Martin.

Top, The New Philadelphia Association organizes the Likes Lecture Series each June to hear from historians, archaeologists, descendants and others on issues related to history and freedom. Gerald McWorter, great-great-grandson of Frank and Lucy McWorter and professor emeritus of African American Studies at the University of Illinois Urbana Champaign, is a frequent speaker. Photo courtesy of Claire Martin.

Bottom left, McWorter descendants and local landowners struck a strong bond with the development of the New Philadelphia project. Allen Kirkpatrick, great-great-grandson of Frank and Lucy and son of Thelma McWorter who grew up in New Philadelphia, center, stands with Larry Armistead, longtime owner and steward of New Philadelphia land, *left*, and one other local helper, *right*. Photo courtesy of Sandra McWorter Marsh.

Bottom right, The 2006 Day of Discovery was held at the Burdick house built in New Philadelphia in 1941. Left to right, Delbert Sheppard, Mary Jo Foster, Dr. Kenwood Foster, Virgil Collins, and Carol McCartney, NPA Secretary, listen to descendant stories. Photo courtesy of Joe Conover.

Top left, Karen Wall and Kate Williams-McWorter scan documents that Karen brought to the 2006 Day of Discovery. Newton, Kansas, genealogist Karen Wallbrought her enormous research notebook on the McWorters. She discovered that her granddaughter was a McWorter and pursued family births, marriages, deaths, and photos from Kansas back to Frank and Lucy.
Top right, The Day of Discovery included a presentation by Ron Carter of Springfield, Illinois, about his New Philadelphia family, the Butlers, who purchased land from "Free Frank" McWorter and worked and socialized with the McWorters. Listening here is Claire Martin, NPA board member and member of the research team, who helped organize the day.
Bottom left, Larry Armistead and his wife Natalie, who died in 2010, farmed in and around New Philadelphia. Larry has provided practical and technical support for each summer whenever needed and continues to live and work adjacent to New Philadelphia.
Bottom right, New Philadelphia descendants Ron and Mary Carter at the Day of Discovery in the Burdick House. Photos this page courtesy of Joe Conover.

Top, *this group portrait of the 2005 New Philadelphia archaeological field school demonstrates the continuity of leadership and the "fresh legs" that came each summer to dig and learn.* ***Front row left to right,*** *Charlotte King, Chris Fennell, Paul Shackel, Terry Martin, Carrie Christman, Christopher Valvano.* ***Back row:*** *Shanique Gibson, Caitlin Bauchat, LaShara Morris, Jordan Bush, Andrea Torvinen, Kimberly Eppler, Jessica Jenkins, Emily Helton, Megan Volkel, and Hannah Mills, who is also a New Philadelphia descendent. Photo courtesy of Paul Shackel.*

Bottom, *The New Philadelphia Association, archaeologists, and one descendant participated in a 2008 Washington, DC public hearing regarding National Landmark Status for the town site. Their testimony helped carry the day for New Philadelphia.* ***Left to right,*** *Phil Bradshaw, Chris Fennell, Linda Bradshaw, Helen Wright, Patricia McWorter, Charlotte King, Paul Shackel, and Carol McCartney. Photo courtesy of Andrea King.*

Top, This editorial cartoon by Bill Beard celebrates July 4th by celebrating local history. One of the achievements of the Interstate 72 Highway Commission was to name a portion of the road after Free Frank. Reproduced with permission of the artist and the Pike Press.

Right, This cover story in Illinois Antiquity, *published by the Illinois Association for the Advancement of Archaeology, was part of a swelling stream of popular and scholarly press coverage of New Philadelphia. A poster version of this cover was the first to commemorate African American sites. It includes Miller Grove, a pre-Civil War community in Pope County Illinois, now within the Shawnee National Forest. The white "milk glass" bottle lid was found at New Philadelphia. Photo by Kate Williams-McWorter.

Top left, This 2006 article in the Pike County Press shows mother and son Pat and Andrew Sprague, owners of Sprague's Kinderhook Lodge, nine miles west of New Philadelphia. The lodge hosted a New Philadelphia exhibit, housed the summer archaeological teams, and sponsors the Likes Lecture Series each June.

Top right, Illinois State Senators Emil Jones and Deanna Demuzio brought a State of Illinois check for $125,000 to help buy New Philadelphia land so that it could become a public and permanent resource. The Pike County Express has a close news record of New Philadelphia since the 1990s, reflecting the fact that the editor Tom Coulson, columnist Carol McCartney, and photographer Pat Likes were each part of NPA.

Bottom, In 2009, thanks to outreach by the NPA and the archaeology team to the National Park Service within the Department of the Interior, New Philadelphia was designated a National Historic Landmark. This article is from the Quincy Herald-Whig, published in Adams County to the north of New Philadelphia. Scan of articles by NPA.

New Philadelphia archeologists impressed by local community

By DAN LONG

"You just don't see people driving up to the site to see what's going on," Courtney Ng said of other excavation sites.

Ng is a college intern working at the New Philadelphia site east of Barry this summer.

The no-longer-existing town was the first incorporated town in the United States by an African American, Free Frank McWorter.

Ng has done other excavations with more population around, but people seldom, if ever, visited those sites. New Philadelphia is different.

"People drive right up and ask what we're doing," Ng said. "We love to talk to them and tell them."

Ng is one of nine college students working at the site who competed with more than 70 undergraduate applicants.

The process brings together students from across the United States of America.

Ng is from Rice University at Houston.

"We're learning about African-American history that's not slavery," she said.

The site will be excavated through June 26, then the team goes to Springfield to evaluate the artifacts gathered.

The team consists of three directors, two graduate supervisors, nine undergraduates, and three graduate student volunteers.

Kati Fay is a graduate student from the University of Illinois, Urbana.

She's been involved since 2004, having been on site that year, 2008, and this year.

"This is my dissertation site," she said. "This site was the reason I changed my major from history to archeology."

Students come from Ohio, New York, Georgia and Iowa.

"It's a very competitive process," George Calfas, graduate supervisor from University of Illinois, Urbana.

In 2008, the team found a to be off the uniform of Civil War button, believed Solomon McWorter, one of Free Frank's sons.

This year, a second button was found.

"We're finding more stoneware this year, too," Calfas said, noting mostly glass has been recovered from the site.

The team is hoping to uncover the foundation of the house of Louisa McWorter, wife of Squire, son of Frank.

Foundation stones have been uncovered, and the team is working to find its dimensions. The house is where several stoneware pieces are being found.

One of the students, Beatrice Adams, is from Alton, but is attending Fisk University in Nashville, TN.

Fisk is where Thelma McWorter Kirkpatrick Wheaton, daughter of Arthur and Ophelia Walker McWorter, started the study of her great-grandfather, Frank, which lead to the book "Free Frank: A Black Pioneer on the Antebellum Frontier" by Juliet Walker, first published in 1983.

Another component of the summer dig is the Marvin J. and Thomas Leo Likes Memorial Lecture Series. This year's theme is "Navigating Landscapes of Struggle and Freedom."

These presentations and discussions will focus on society's commitment to struggles for freedom in the past and present, efforts to achieve the unattained promises of democracy, and the heritage of social networks and communities in the 19th and 20th centuries shaped by the same challenges Frank McWorter and Abraham Lincoln confronted in their lifetimes.

The heritage of Frank McWorter, who founded the integrated community of New Philadelphia in 1836, and the legacies of the residents of that town, provide lessons that parallel challenges confronted by Lincoln at a national scale. New Philadelphia was designated a National Historic Landmark in the bicentennial year of Lincoln's birth.

The speaker series is sponsored by the New Philadelphia Association, with the cooperation of Sprague's Kinderhook Lodge and Illinois State Museum.

The presentations and discussions include the following events, which will be at Kinderhook Lodge, 22168 State Highway 106, Barry, Illinois 62312, phone 217-432-1090; or Illinois State Museum's Research Collections Center, 1011 East Ash Street, Springfield, Illinois 62703, phone 217-782-6695.

Additional details and driving directions for the Kinderhook Lodge, between the towns of Kinderhook and Barry on Rt. 106, are available on at: http://www.kinderhooklodge.com.

Upcoming lectures:
+ June 15, "Local History, National Identity: Why Heritage Matters in the 21st Century". Presented by Paul A. Shackel, Kinderhook Lodge.
+ June 22, "Putting the Community in 'Community Archaeology'". Presented by Anna Agbe-Davies, Kinderhook Lodge.
+ June 29, "Stealing Away: Ingenuity and Strategy in the Paths from Slavery to Freedom". Presented by Terry Ransom and Christopher Fennell, Illinois State Museum.
+ July 6, "Struggling for Freedom: Landscape by the Women, Men, and Children Escaping Bondage". Presented by Rebecca Ginsburg, Illinois State Museum.
+ July 14, "Geological Adventures on the Carolina Frontier: The Search for Kaolin and the Rise of a Heroic African-American Potter", Presented by John Michael Vlach, Illinois State Museum.

SEDRIE HART AND KEISHAIA GRIFFITH (right) trowel away layers of dirt while Terry Martin (back) sifts dirt, looking for artifacts at the New Philadelphia site east of Barry.
PHOTO BY DAN LONG

ILLINOIS RURAL ELECTRIC COOPERATIVE

New Philadelphia site gets boost

Co-op's 10-year pledge will help raise public appeal of project to preserve community platted by Free Frank McWorter

By DEBORAH GERTZ HUSAR
Herald-Whig Staff Writer

BARRY, Ill. — A financial pledge will mean some big changes at a Pike County site boasting plenty of history but little for people to see.

New Philadelphia "basically is a farm field with some cabins moved in, not original but of the era," New Philadelphia Association President Phil Bradshaw said.

But Bradshaw hopes to see a visitors kiosk and the beginnings of a walking trail in place by June thanks to financial support from Illinois Rural Electric Cooperative announced Monday afternoon. The Winchester-based co-op pledged $7,500 each year for 10 years to develop physical structures and improvements at the historic site.

Cooperative General Manager Bruce Giffin and board members "felt an investment in this project would go a long ways in helping the local economic potential in the long run, the organization, and help develop the site," said Shawn Rennecker, the cooperative's economic development director.

The co-op's donation will be leveraged by support from John Wood Community College through in-kind labor through its construction trades program.

"Any additional leverage that could be secured based off the resources we have

See SITE, Page 9A

New Philadelphia Association President Phil Bradshaw, left, accepts a $7,500 check from Jim Gay of the Illinois Rural Electric Cooperative Monday afternoon in the Burdick Center at the New Philadelphia Historic Site near Baylis. (H-W Photo/Phil Carlson)

Top, *The dig generated lots of local interest, which was welcomed. This affirmed the transition from memory to rebirth of the town.*
Bottom, *The Illinois Rural Electric Cooperative became a strong financial supporter of the New Philadelphia project with a 10-year commitment of $7,500 each year beginning in 2012. Here Jim Gay presents a check to Phil Bradshaw at an NPA meeting at the Burdick House in New Philadelphia. Scan of articles by NPA.*

Top, *John Wood Community College instructor Dan Arnsman instructs students completing a large kiosk, or shed, for visitors to New Philadelphia. Photo used with permission of the Illinois Rural Electric Cooperative.*
Right, *The Living Museum, magazine of the Illinois State Museum, published a special issue on the first 10 years of the New Philadelphia archaeological project.* **Clockwise from left to right**, *a number of participants in the 2011 excavations: Annalies Morris, Joseph Tonelli, Kaila Akina, Terry Martin, Joe Hogan, Jeff Amerson, Thomas Glantz, Mary Kathryn Rocheford, Chris Fennell, Miriam Manda, Amanda Burtt, Hillary Christopher, Shawn Fields, Antoinette West, and Elizabeth Usherwood. Scan of magazine cover by New Philadelphia Association.*

Top, This 2010 group portrait of McWorter descendants was taken on the porch of the Burdick House in New Philadelphia. **Seated, left to right,** Doña Fleur Wells, Sandra McWorter Marsh, Evelyn Leola Parks, Shirley McWorter Moss, Lonie Wilson, and Gretchen Wells. **Standing, left to right,** Vincent Vann, Lloyd "Bobby" Vann, Kevin Vann, Gerald McWorter.

Bottom, This portrait was taken in Ventura, California on a visit to descendants of Squire McWorter, who was born soon after Frank purchased Lucy's freedom. **Front row**, Karen Hamilton-McWorter, Patricia McWorter, Gerald A. McWorter, and Jerry McWorter. **Back row,** Jennie McWorter; blues musician Jerry McWorter; and Kathy McWorter. Kathy wrote the screenplay for The War, a movie about rural kids facing down racism. Photos by Kate Williams-McWorter.

One hundred years after a small friendship album was given by New Philadelphia School teacher Miss Carrie to student Gerald Arnett, Mary Kay Arnett brought it to Gerald McWorter. It contained another New Philadelphia school photo and a list of the 1916-1917 "scholars," Gerald Arnett, Lillie Booth, Alvin Burdick, Everett, Pearl, Neal, Naomi, and Lloyd Gibson; Erma Hull, Ellen McWorter, Cora Siefers, and Geneva, Manford, Leonard, Frankie, and Ernest Venicombe. School photo courtesy of Mary Kay Arnett; photo by Kate Williams-McWorter.

Epilogue

This book connects the dots, putting together a narrative of New Philadelphia based on documents, photographs of people and places identified or not, and the stories maintained as oral history. It is an act of historical imagination, a narrative for the collective evaluation by descendants and people with historical interest in such a place.

This book comes out at a time in the history of the United States that challenges everyone to rethink the history of the country and the experiment it has posed in its struggle for democracy. From the perspective of the native peoples and African Americans, as well as all other oppressed and exploited peoples, the struggle for democracy continues and at times does not seem to be imminent. The slogan "Make America great again" must be seen alongside the Langston Hughes poem quoted at the start of the book: "O, let America be America again—The land that never has been yet—And yet must be—the land where *every* man is free."

New Philadelphia is a small place with a big story, a glimpse of what might happen in this country if the racism and negation of the numerous patterns of unity across all ethnic communities were to be curtailed and eliminated. We have often said if New Philadelphia was possible, then maybe America is possible. The greatness we want has never been, but we hope New Philadelphia gives a suggestion of what is possible.

Black people, and all working and poor people, don't have a vested interest in maintaining the usual that has been for the last few hundred years. Yet in spite of the problems inherent in the larger society, there has been much to celebrate, and we can stand on this to move forward.

Appendix

We acknowledge here all the student archaeologists who helped in the rebirth of New Philadelphia, and the members of the 1836 Club, who have donated to the New Philadelphia Association as of October 2017. We also provide a list of artifacts from New Philadelphia that are in the Smithsonian Institution in Washington DC, as of February 2018.

Student archaeologists 2004-2011

2004 National Science Foundation (NSF) Interns
Cecilia Ayala
Dana Blount
Megan Cerasale
Richard Fairly
Kathryn Fay
Steve Manion
Jesse Sloan
Janel Vasallo
Laura Wardwell

2004 Graduate Students
Carrie Christman
Charlotte King
William White

2005 University of Illinois Undergraduate Field School Students
Alison Azzarello
Michael Collart
Elizabeth Davis
Thomas Duggan
Maria Elana Frias
Hillary Iden
Kyle Johnson
Matthew Kane
Gail Kirk
Christina Puzzo
Leslie Salyers
Jill Scott
Liz Watts
Charles Williams

2005 NSF Interns
Caitlin Bauchat
Kimberly Eppler
Shanique Gibson
Emily Helton
Jessica Jenkins
Hannah Mills (New Philadelphia descendant)
LaShara Morris
Andrea Torvinen
Megan Volkel

2005 Graduate Students
Carrie Christman
Charlotte King
Christopher Valvano

2006 NSF Interns
Adeola Adegbola
Holly Brookens
Athena Hsieh
Jason Jacoby
Hillary Livingston
Angie Maranville
Maria Nieves Colon
Shamia Sandels
Erin Smith

2006 Graduate Students
Charlotte King
Christopher Valvano

2008 NSF Interns
Joshua Brown
George Calfas
Shalonda Collins
Mathew Davila
Kathrine Hardcastle
Alison McCartan
Annelise Morris
Elizabeth Sylak
Camille Sumter

2008 Graduate Students
Megan Bailey
Kathryn Fay
Christopher Valvano

2010 NSF Interns
Beatrice Adams
Meaghan Alston
Keishaia Griffith
Sedrie Hart
Courtney Ng
John Schultz
Tyquin Washington
Margaret Wolf
Tyrell Yarbrough

2010 Graduate Students
George Calfas
Kathryn Fay
Mary Kathryn Rocheford
Blair Starnes

2011 NSF Interns
Kaila Akina
Shawn Fields
Joseph Tonelli
Amanda Burtt
Thomas Glantz
Elizabeth Usherwood
Hillary Christopher
Miriam Manda
Antoinette West

2011 Graduate Students
Kathryn Fay
Annelise Morris
Mary Kathryn Rocheford

Members of the New Philadelphia Association's 1836 Club as of April 2018

These individuals and organizations purchased a virtual town lot for $1,000, or if asterisked two lots for $1,836.

In Memory of Natalie Armistead
City of Barry
Philip and Linda Bradshaw
Central State Bank-Kinderhook with Brian Nation
Coffman Family—In memory of Clarence and Irene Coffman
Joe and Janet Conover*
Jerry and Marynel Corton
Glen "Bush" and Lillian Robb Crump Family
Craig C. Culver
Terrell and Vicki Dempsey
Brian and Dr. Mary Iftner Dobbins
Descendants of the James M. Doran Family
Dr. Kathryn Fay
Mark Field and the Farmers Bank of Liberty-Barry*
Dr. Kenwood Foster
Beth Gates-Warren and Bob Boghosian
Bruce and Kay Giffin
Gully and Hechler Insurance Company
Rodger and Bonnie Hannel*
Wayne Hazelrigg
David and Kaye Iftner*
Charlotte King*
Romona Hart Levy
Pat Likes
Harold and Mary Lee Crump
Lister Family
Dr. Terrance Martin and Claire Martin*
Carol McCartney
Richard McTucker and Debbie Harshman Families
Gerald McWorter and Kate Williams-McWorter*
Nancy and Tom Mills Family*
McCarl-Morrow Family
New Philadelphia Archaeology Teams
Wayne Riley
Dr. Paul Shackel and Dr. Barbara Little
John and Elaine Shover Family
Kelly Syrcle*
Patrick and Audrey Syrcle
Friends honoring James Washington, his grandson LeMoyne Washington, and Family*
Harry and Helen Wright*

Other institutional funders include Central State Bank, Community Foundation Serving West Central Illinois & Northeast Missouri, Farmers Bank of Liberty, Illinois Rural Electric Cooperative, and Quincy Medical Group.

Artifacts from New Philadelphia in the Smithsonian Institution

Numerical codes for artifacts indicate where in New Philadelphia the item was found and who owned the land at that time.

Items on loan from the Illinois State Museum to the Museum of American History, Washington, D.C.

Charlotte Cowan receipt. Pike County Courthouse, to be re-photographed by Doug Carr.

Civil War Button. NP#699.037, Block 13, Lot 3, EU 11, Level A2. Landowner: Arnett.

Ceramic Cup. Refitted from NP#824.028, 818.030, 818.031, 824.039, 824.040, 827.002, & 827.003. Block 13, Lot 4, EU 16, Level B3. Landowner: Arnett.

Writing Slate Fragment and Pencil Fragments (2). Writing slate fragment, NP#489.088, Block 8, Lot 2, Fea 14, Level a4. Landowner: Archaeological Conservancy. Slate pencil fragment, NP 491.046, Block 3, Lot 7, EU 9, Level A1. Landowner: Archaeological Conservancy. Slate pencil fragment, NP 413.042, Block 3, Lot 7, EU 3, Level B1. Landowner: Archaeological Conservancy.

Marbles (2). White ceramic marble, NP#38.53, Block 9, Lot 5, EU 2, Level F1a1. Landowner: Archaeological Conservancy. Blue, white and brown Bennington marble, NP#12.38, Block 3, Lot 4, EU 2, Level A1. Landowner: Archaeological Conservancy.

Patent Medicine Bottles (3). Brown glass bottle & fragments, NP#798.099 & 798.110, Block 13, Lot 4, EU 14, Lv B1. Landowner: Arnett. Aqua glass "Dr King's New Discovery" bottle, NP# 798.317, Block 13, Lot 4, EU 14, Level B1, Feature 12. Landowner: Arnett. Aqua glass medicine/condiment bottle, NP#463.011, Block 3, Lot 7, EU 7, Level STR B3. Landowner: Archaeological Conservancy.

"Turk's Head" Pipe Fragment. NP#489.107, Block 8, Lot 2, Feature 14, Level a4. Landowner: Archaeological Conservancy.

Lice Comb. NP#38.61, Block 9, Lot 5, EU 2, Level F1a1. Landowner: Archaeological Conservancy.

Clothing Buckle. NP#164.67, Block 13, Lot 3, EU 3, Level A2. Landowner: Arnett.

Thimbles (2). NP#21.45, Block 9, Lot 5, EU 2, Level A3. Landowner: Archaeological Conservancy. NP#38.46, Block 9, Lot 5, EU 2, Level F1a1. Landowner: Archaeological Conservancy.

Pig Bone. Sus scrofa mandible, NP#489, Block 8, Lot 2, Feature 14. Landowner: Archaeological Conservancy.

Cow Bones (4). Bos taurus atlas vertebra, NP#799, Block 13, Lot 4, Level B1, Feature 12. Landowner: Arnett. Bos taurus ilium fragment(R), NP#479, Block 8, Lot 2, Feature 14. Landowner: Archaeological Conservancy. Bos taurus scapula fragment (L), NP#434, Block 3, Lot 7, EU 6, Level A1. Landowner: Archaeological Conservancy. Bos taurus rib, NP#593, Block 7, Lot 1, EU 5, Level A4. Landowner: Arnett.

> Items on loan from McWorter descendants to the
> Museum of American History, Washington, D.C.

Solomon McWorter's basin and pitcher
Child's chair made by Solomon McWorter
Numerous photographs

> Items on loan from or gifted by
> McWorter descendants and others
> to the Museum of African American
> History and Culture, Washington, D.C.

Bronze bust of Frank McWorter by Shirley McWorter Moss
Book: *Introduction to African American Studies* by Gerald McWorter/ Abdul Alkalimat (gifted by Bertha Maxwell Roddey)

Works Consulted

Unlike a book aimed at academics or researchers, this book is not formally footnoted. This is to keep it accessible to a general reader. The published sources that we used are listed here. We also used material in archives, in other family collections, and in our own family collection. We hope to move our collection to an institution so that others can go to the same information and photographs and advance knowledge about this remarkable town and family. Oral history—stories told and retold to us through the decades—is also part of this book. We encourage readers to preserve their family and local oral histories in whatever way possible. Libraries and archives near you can help with this.

Websites

New Philadelphia Association
   http://newphiladelphiail.org/

McWorter Family
   http://www.mcworter.net/

Free Frank
   http://www.freefrank.org/

The National Museum of American History
   http://americanhistory.si.edu/many-voices-exhibition/peopling-expanding-nation-1776%E2%80%931900/western-migration/free-frank-mcworter

National Park Service
   https://www.nps.gov/Nr/twhp/wwwlps/lessons/130newphila/index.htm

Prairie Fire: Free Frank and New Philadelphia (WILL-TV)
   https://www.youtube.com/watch?v=WIin2ATrnDI

Time Team America (PBS Video)
   http://www.pbs.org/time-team/explore-the-sites/new-philadelphia/

University of Maryland
http://www.heritage.umd.edu/chrsweb/new%20philadelphia/newphiladelphia.htm

University of Illinois
http://faculty.las.illinois.edu/cfennell/NP/

Wikipedia
https://en.wikipedia.org/wiki/New_Philadelphia_Town_Site

"3 Oct 1990, Page 4 - The Courier-Journal at Newspapers.com." *Newspapers.com*. Accessed April 6, 2018. http://www.newspapers.com/image/110004162/?terms=juliet%2Bwalker%2Bdescendant. Login required.

8th Grade American History class, Chardon Middle School, Chardon, Ohio. "How Many Signers of the Declaration of Independence Owned Slaves?" Accessed April 6, 2018. http://www.mrheintz.com/how-many-signers-of-the-declaration-of-independence-owned-slaves.html.

Aero Service Corp. *AR 2 140*. Scale approximately 1:20,000. [Flight of Pike County, Illinois]. Washington, D.C.: U.S. Department of Agriculture, Soil Conservation Service, 1936.

Agbe-Davies, Anna S. 2010. "Foreword: An Engaged Archaeology for Our Mutual Benefit: The Case of New Philadelphia." *Historical Archaeology* 44, no. 1: 1–6.

Agbe-Davies, Anna S., and Claire Fuller Martin. 2013. "'Demanding a Share of Public Regard': African American Education at New Philadelphia, Illinois." *Transforming Anthropology* 21, no. 2 (October): 103–21.

Alkalimat, Abdul (Gerald A. McWorter) and Associates. 1986. *Introduction to Afro-American Studies: A Peoples College Primer*. 6th edition. Chicago: Twenty-First Century Books and Publications. Accessed on April 6, 2018 at http://alkalimat.org/writings.html

Andrews, E. Benjamin. 1895. *History of the United States*, Volume III. New York: Charles Scribner's Sons.

Arnold, Isaac Newton. 1866. *The History of Abraham Lincoln, and the

Overthrow of Slavery. Chicago: Clarke and Co.

Bangert, Heather. 2015. "Once Upon and Time in Quincy: Black Abolitionist Network Grew with City." *Quincy Herald-Whig*, January 11, 2015. Accessed April 6, 2018. http://www.whig.com/story/27820292/once-upon-a-time-in-quincy-black-abolistionist-network-grew-with-city

Barry Historical Museum. 2016. *Barry (IL) Family Histories: Histories of Local Pioneers*. Liberty, Illinois: Elliott Publishing, Inc.

Beasley, Joy, and Tom Gwaltney. 2010. "New Philadelphia Pedestrian Survey: Phase I Investigations at an Historic Town Site." *Historical Archaeology* 44, no. 1: 20–42.

de Beaumont, Gustave. 1958. *Marie; Or, Slavery in the United States: A Novel of Jacksonian America*. Stanford: Stanford University Press. First published in French in 1835.

Bennett, Lerone. 2001. *Forced into Glory: Abraham Lincoln's White Dream*. Chicago: Johnson Publishing Company.

Black Hawk. 1834. *Life of Ma-ka-tai-me-she-kia-kiak or Black Hawk*. Boston: Russell, Odiorne & Metcalf. Accessed April 6, 2018 at https://hdl.handle.net/2027/mdp.39015060799189

Bradford, Sarah H. 1886. *Harriet, the Moses of Her People*. 2nd ed. New York: George R. Lockwood & Son. Accessed April 6, 2018. http://hdl.handle.net/2027/nc01.ark:/13960/t5hb07r8w.

Buchanan, Thomas C. 2004. *Black Life on the Mississippi: Slaves, Free Blacks, and the Western Steamboat World*. Chapel Hill: University of North Carolina Press.

Burdick, Lorraine. 1992. New Philadelphia: Where I Lived. Unpublished paper.

Cahill, Emmett. 1996. *The Shipmans of East Hawai'i*. Honolulu: University of Hawai'i Press.

Cha-Jua, Sundiata Keita. 2000. *America's First Black Town: Brooklyn, Illinois, 1830-1915*. Urbana: University of Illinois Press.

Christman, Carrie A. 2010. "Voices of New Philadelphia: Memories and Stories of the People and Place." *Historical Archaeology* 44, no. 1: 102–11. The oral histories that Christman collected are also available at http://www.heritage.umd.edu/chrsweb/

New Philadelphia/oralhistories.htm

Ciotta, Jennifer. 2007. "A Revealing Interview with Terrell Dempsey, Author of *Searching for Jim: Slavery in Sam Clemens's World*. Literary Traveler." Posted January 30, 2017. Accessed April 6, 2018. http://www.literarytraveler.com/articles/terrell_dempsey_twain/

Coffin, Levi. 1880. *Reminiscences of Levi Coffin*. Second edition. Cincinnati: Robert Clarke 7 Co. Accessed April 6, 2018 at http://docsouth.unc.edu/nc/coffin/coffin.html

Cooke, Sarah, and Rachel Ramadhyani. 1993. *Indians and a Changing Frontier: The Art of George Winter*. Indianapolis: Indiana Historical Society, in cooperation with the Tippecanoe County Historical Association.

"The Deep Snow: Winter of 1830-31 Has Legends That Chicago's Records Fail to Shake." 1968. *Illinois Intelligencer (Published as Part of the Illinois Sesquicentennial)* 150, no. 15 (January 28): 1, 3. Accessed April 6, 2018. http://www.illinoishistory.com/deepsnow.htm.

Dempsey, Terrell. 2013. *Searching for Jim: Slavery in Sam Clemens's World*. Columbia: University of Missouri Press.

Drew, Benjamin. 1856. *A North-side View of Slavery: The Refugee, or, The Narratives of Fugitive Slaves in Canada Related by Themselves: With an Account of the History and Condition of the Colored Population of Upper Canada*. Boston: John P. Jewett and Co. Reprinted in 2004 as *Refugees from Slavery: Autobiographies of Fugitive Slaves in Canada*. Mineola, New York: Dover Publications.

Drotning, Phillip T. 1968. *An American Traveler's Guide to Black History*. Garden City, New York: Doubleday.

Drury, John. 1955. *This is Pike County, Illinois; an up-to-date historical narrative with county and township maps and many unique aerial photographs of cities, towns, villages and farmsteads*. The American aerial county history series: Illinois no. 6. Chicago: The Loree Company.

Eckberg, Carl J. 1998. *French Roots in the Illinois Country: The Mississippi Frontier in Colonial Times*. Urbana: University of Illinois Press.

———. 2007. *Stealing Indian Women: Native Slavery in the Illinois Country.* Urbana: University of Illinois Press.

Emerson, Louis E., compiler. 1919. *Counties of Illinois: their origin and evolution; with twenty-three maps showing the original and present boundary lines of each county of the state.* Springfield, Illinois: Illinois State Journal Co.

Ensign, D. W. 1872. *Atlas Map of Pike County, Illinois.* Davenport, Iowa: Andreas, Lyter & Co.

Evans, Bob, Charles A. Francis, and Pike County Historical Society. 2014. *Pike County Illinois History and Families 1821-2014.* Morley, Missouri: Acclaim Press.

Fennell, Christopher C. 2010. "Damaging Detours: Routes, Racism, and New Philadelphia." *Historical Archaeology* 44, no. 1: 138–54.

———. 2017. *Broken Chains and Subverted Plans: Ethnicity, Race, and Commodities.* Gainesville: University Press of Florida.

———. 2011. "Examining Structural Racism in Jim Crow-Era Illinois." In *The Materiality of Freedom: Archaeologies of Post-Emancipation Life*, edited by Jodi A. Barnes., 175–89. Columbia, South Caroline: University of South Carolina Press.

Fischer, Leroy H. 1968. "Lincoln's 1858 Visit to Pittsfield, Illinois." *Journal of the Illinois State Historical Society* 61, no. 3: 350–64.

Grimshaw, William A. 1876. *History of Pike County A Centennial Address Delivered by Hon. William A. Grimshaw, at Pittsfield, Pike County, Illinois, July 4, 1876.* Pittsfield, Illinois: Democrat Job Rooms.

Gutman, Ari. 2015. "Dr. Richard Eells Impact on the Underground Railroad in Quincy: A Paper for Junior History Fair," Accessed April 6, 2018. https://akibahistoryfair.files.wordpress.com/2015/03/eells-ari-gutman.docx.

Hargrave, Michael L. 2010. "Geophysical Detection of Features and Community Plan at New Philadelphia, Illinois." *Historical Archaeology* 44, no. 1: 43–57.

Helton, Emily G. 2010. "Education and Gender in New Philadelphia." *Historical Archaeology* 44, no. 1: 112–24.

Hemphill, C. Dallett. 2014. *Siblings: Brothers and Sisters in American History*. Oxford, UK: Oxford University Press.

History of Pike County, Illinois : Together with Sketches of Its Cities, Villages and Townships, Educational, Religious, Civil, Military, and Political History, Portraits of Prominent Persons and Biographies of Representative Citizens. History of Illinois, Embracing Accounts of Pre-Historic Races, Aborigines, French, English and American Conquests, and a General Review of Its Civil, Political and Military History; History of Illinois...; Digest of State Laws. 1880. Chicago: C. C. Chapman & Company.

History of Tazewell County, Illinois: Together with Sketches of Its Cities, Villages and Townships, Educational, Religious, Civil, Military, and Political History; Portraits of Prominent Persons and Biographies of Representative Citizens; History of Illinois...; Digest of State Laws. 1879. Chicago: C. C. Chapman & Company.

Hughes, Langston. 1938. *A New Song*. New York: International Workers Order.

King, Charlotte. No date. "New Philadelphia: A Multi-Racial Town on the Illinois Frontier" National Park Service Lesson Plans. Accessed April 6, 2018. https://www.nps.gov/Nr/twhp/wwwlps/lessons/130newphila/index.htm

———. 2003. Passed by Time: American's All-Black Towns. Unpublished undergraduate thesis, University of Maryland College Park.

———. 2006. New Philadelphia Census Data. University of Maryland Center for Heritage Resource Studies, College Park, MD. College Park. Accessed April 6, 2018 at http://www.heritage.umd.edu/chrsweb/new%20philadelphia/New%20Philadelphia/censusfiles/CensusDataMenu.htm

———. 2010. "Separated by Death and Color: The African American Cemetery of New Philadelphia, Illinois." *Historical Archaeology* 44, no. 1: 125–37.

———. 2012. New Philadelphia on the Route to Freedom. A pamphlet. Barry, Illinois: New Philadelphia Association. September 13.

Landrum, Carl A. 1986. *Historical Sketches of Quincy Illinois*. Rev. ed. Quincy, Illinois: Historical Society of Quincy and Adams County.

———. 1966. *Quincy in the Civil War a View of the Great Conflict as Seen through the Eyes of a Quincy Historian*. 1st ed. Quincy, Illinois: Historical Society of Quincy and Adams County.

LaRoche, Cheryl Janifer. 2014, *Free Black Communities and the Underground Railroad: The Geography of Resistance*. Champaign: University of Illinois Press.

Laws of the State of Illinois passed by the tenth general assembly at their session commencing December 5, 1836 and ending March 6, 1837. 1837. Vandalia, Illinois: Williams Walters, Public Printer.

Lenstra, Noah. 2009. The African-American mining experience in Illinois from 1800 to 1920. Unpublished monograph. Accessed April 6, 2018. http://hdl.handle.net/2142/9578

Likes, Pat. No date. Faces of New Philadelphia: A study of Pioneer Settlement in Frontier Illinois. Pamphlet accompanying a set of photographs. Barry, Illinois: New Philadelphia Association.

Mackenzie, Dana. 2005. "Ahead of Its Time?" *Smithsonian* 35, no. 10: 28–29.

Main, Josiah. 1915. *The Agriculture of Pike County, Illinois*. Ithaca, N.Y.: Published by the author. Accessed April 6, 2018. http://books.google.com/books?id=miQxAQAAMAAJ

Martin, Claire Fuller, and Terrance J. Martin. 2010. "Agriculture and Regionalism at New Philadelphia." *Historical Archaeology* 44, no. 1: 72–84.

Martin, Terrance J., and Claire Fuller Martin. 2010. "Courtly, Careful, Thrifty: Subsistence and Regional Origin at New Philadelphia." *Historical Archaeology* 44, no. 1: 85–101.

Martin, Terrance, Paul Shackel, and Christopher Fennell. 2004. "New Philadelphia: The XYZs of the First Excavations." *The Living Museum* 66, no. 4 (Winter): 8–13.

Matteson, Grace E. and Pike County Historical Society. 1964."Free

Frank" McWorter and the Town of Philadelphia, Pike County, Illinois. Pittsfield, Illinois: Pike County Historical Society.

McKenney, Thomas Loraine and James Hall. 1848. *History of the Indian Tribes of North America, with Biographical Sketches and Anecdotes, of the Principal Chiefs*. Volume 1. Philadelphia: J. T. Bowen.

McWhirter, Alan D. "McWh*rter Genealogy; Page on John McWhorter." Accessed March 11, 2017. http://homepages.rootsweb.ancestry.com/~mcwgen/johnva.htm#Frank%20McWorter.

McWorter, Gerald A. (Abdul Alkalimat). 2010. "Comment: Conditions of Subject and Object." *Historical Archaeology* 44, no. 1: 155–57.

Miller, Edward A. 1998. *The Black Civil War Soldiers of Illinois: The Story of the Twenty-Ninth U.S. Colored Infantry*. Columbia, South Carolina: University of South Carolina Press.

Morgan, Ted. 1996. *Shovel of Stars: The Making of the American West 1800 to the Present*. New York: Simon and Schuster.

Morris, Annelise. 2009. "Religion, Social Networks, and Temperance in New Philadelphia, Illinois." Department of Anthropology undergraduate research paper, University of Illinois.

King, Charlotte. No date. "New Philadelphia: A Multi-Racial Town on the Illinois Frontier" National Park Service Lesson Plans. Accessed April 6, 2018. https://www.nps.gov/Nr/twhp/wwwlps/lessons/130newphila/index.htm

Park Aerial Surveys, Inc. *AR-4JJ-35*. Scale approximately 1:20,000. Invitation no. ASCS-4-68 DC. Item 2. [Flight of Pike County, Illinois]. Washington, D.C.: U.S. Department of Agriculture, Agricultural Stabilization and Conservation Service, 1968.

Payne, Jon. 2011. *One Boy's Pike County*. Clarendon Hills, Illinois: Floodplains Publishing.

Pike County Historical Society. 2014. *Pike County Illinois: History and Families*. Morley, Missouri: Acclaim Press.

"Pike County, Illinois 1872 Atlas - Lowe Family Descendants." Accessed January 6, 2017. http://www.lowefamilydescendants.com/Home/houseoflow-e-mainpage/pike-county-illinois-1872-atlas.

Pike County Natives, Teachers, Former School Students, and Interested Citizens, sponsored by the Pike County Historical Society, Pittsfield, Illinois and prepared by Roma McConnell Weir. 1999. *Pike County Illinois Schools 1823-1995: History and Pictures*. Mt. Vernon, Indiana: Windmill Publications, Inc.

Pinkowski, Jennifer. 2005. "Integrating the Frontier." *Archaeology* 58, no. 5: 42–47.

"Pulaski Co, KY African American Research Project - Slaves in Court Records." Accessed March 12, 2017. http://kykinfolk.org/pulaski/poc/trans.html.

Rose, James A. *Counties of Illinois: their origin and evolution*. Springfield, Illinois: Secretary of State's Office, 1906.

Savage, Beth L, Carol D. Shull, United States National Park Service, National Conference of State Historic Preservation Officers, and National Register of Historic Places. 1994. *African American Historic Places*. Washington, D.C.: Preservation Press.

Shackel, Paul A. 2005. "Local Identity, National Memory, and Heritage Tourism: Creating a Sense of Place with Archaeology." *Illinois Antiquity* 40, no. 3 (September): 24–27.

———. 2010. "Identity and Collective Action in a Multiracial Community." *Historical Archaeology* 44, no. 1: 58–71.

———. 2010. "Introduction: Remembering New Philadelphia." *Historical Archaeology* 44, no. 1: 7–19.

———. 2011. *New Philadelphia: An Archaeology of Race in the Heartland*. Berkeley: University of California Press.

———. 2011. "America's Home Town: Fiction, Mark Twain, and the Re-Creation of Hannibal, Missouri." *International Journal of Heritage Studies* 17, no. 3: 197–213.

Shackel, Paul A., Terrance J. Martin, Joy D. Beasley and Tom Gwaltney. 2004. "Rediscovering New Philadelphia: Race and Racism on the Illinois Frontier," *Illinois Antiquity* (March).

Simpson, Helen McWorter. 1981. *Makers of History*. Evansville, Indiana: L.B. Warren.

Smardz Frost, Karolyn. 2007. *I've Got a Home in Gloryland: A Lost*

Tale of the Underground Railroad. New York: Farrar, Strauss and Giroux.

Spielmaker, Debra. 2005. Growing a Nation: The Story of American Agriculture. North Logan, Utah: LetterPress Software. Accessed April 6, 2018. https://www.agclassroom.org/gan/timeline/farmers_land.htm

Standard Atlas of Pike County, Illinois : Including a Plat Book of the Villages, Cities and Townships of the County. 1912. Chicago: Ogle.

Sterling, Dorothy. 1991. *Ahead of Her Time: Abby Kelley and the Politics of Anti-Slavery*. New York: W.W. Norton.

Teague, Tom. 2002. "From Farrakhan to New Philadelphia: Vibert White Embraces History at Every Crossroad." *Illinois Heritage* 5, no. 2 (April): 6–10.

Thompson, Jess M. 1967. *Pike County History, as Printed in Installments in the Pike County Republican, Pittsfield, Illinois, 1935-1939*. Racine, Wisconsin: Preston Miller.

de Tocqueville, Alexis. 1899. *Democracy in America, Volume 1*. Translated by Henry Reeve. New York: Colonial Press. Originally published in English in 1838. Accessed April 6, 2018. http://xroads.virginia.edu/~HYPER/DETOC/.

"Trail of Tears." Accessed April 6, 2018. http://www.cherokee.org/AboutTheNation/History/TrailofTears.aspx.

Twain, Mark. *Adventures of Huckleberry Finn*. 1885. New York: Charles L. Webster and Company.

Turner, Glennette Tilley. 2001. *The Underground Railroad in Illinois*. Glen Ellyn, Illinois: Newman Educational Publishing.

U. S. Census Bureau. "1850 Census: The Seventh Census of the United States." Accessed December 22, 2016. https://www.census.gov/library/publications/1853/dec/1850a.html.

Walker, Juliet E. K. 1983. "Pioneer Slave Entrepreneurship-Patterns, Processes, and Perspectives: The Case of the Slave Free Frank on the Kentucky Pennyroyal, 1795-1819." *The Journal of Negro History* 68, no. 3: 289–308.

———. 1983. *Free Frank: A Black Pioneer on the Antebellum Frontier*. Lexington, Kentucky: University Press of Kentucky.

———. 1985. "Entrepreneurial Ventures in the Origin of Nineteenth-Century Agricultural Towns: Pike County, 1823-1880." *Illinois Historical Journal* 78, no. 1: 45–64.

———. 1986. "Racism, Slavery, and Free Enterprise: Black Entrepreneurship in the United States before the Civil War." *The Business History Review* 60, no. 3: 343–82.

Watkins, Hollis. 2015. *Brother Hollis: The Sankofa of a Movement Man*. Clinton, Mississippi: Sankofa Publishing.

Watkins, Sylvestre C., and A. Lincoln. 1963. "Some of Early Illinois' Free Negroes." *Journal of the Illinois State Historical Society* 56, no. 3: 495–507.

"Which U.S. Presidents Owned Slaves?" Accessed April 6, 2018. http://www.nathanielturner.com/whichpresidentsownedslaves.htm.

Wyman, Mark. 1990. *Immigration History and Ethnicity in Illinois: A Guide*. Springfield, Illinois: Illinois State Historical Society.